CAMBRIDGE LIBRARY COLLECTION

Books of enduring scholarly value

Classics

From the Renaissance to the nineteenth century, Latin and Greek were compulsory subjects in almost all European universities, and most early modern scholars published their research and conducted international correspondence in Latin. Latin had continued in use in Western Europe long after the fall of the Roman empire as the lingua franca of the educated classes and of law, diplomacy, religion and university teaching. The flight of Greek scholars to the West after the fall of Constantinople in 1453 gave impetus to the study of ancient Greek literature and the Greek New Testament. Eventually, just as nineteenth-century reforms of university curricula were beginning to erode this ascendancy, developments in textual criticism and linguistic analysis, and new ways of studying ancient societies, especially archaeology, led to renewed enthusiasm for the Classics. This collection offers works of criticism, interpretation and synthesis by the outstanding scholars of the nineteenth century.

Hellenistic Military & Naval Developments

First published in 1930, this is a collection of essays by the noted classical scholar W. W. Tarn, originally delivered as Lees Knowles Lectures in Military History at Trinity College, Cambridge. Tarn draws on a range of sources to trace the history and development of warfare in the Hellenistic period, with particular emphasis on military strategy under Alexander the Great. The first lecture outlines the role of infantry, analysing the weaponry used in various battles. In the second lecture, Tarn examines the development of cavalry, its history in Macedonia, Thessaly and Iran, and its use of elephants and camels. The final lecture explores improvements in siege and naval methods, with particular attention to advancements in artillery. Providing valuable insight into a period of extensive military innovation, this book gives an overview of the military and naval arts and sciences of the Hellenistic era.

T0382403

Cambridge University Press has long been a pioneer in the reissuing of out-of-print titles from its own backlist, producing digital reprints of books that are still sought after by scholars and students but could not be reprinted economically using traditional technology. The Cambridge Library Collection extends this activity to a wider range of books which are still of importance to researchers and professionals, either for the source material they contain, or as landmarks in the history of their academic discipline.

Drawing from the world-renowned collections in the Cambridge University Library, and guided by the advice of experts in each subject area, Cambridge University Press is using state-of-the-art scanning machines in its own Printing House to capture the content of each book selected for inclusion. The files are processed to give a consistently clear, crisp image, and the books finished to the high quality standard for which the Press is recognised around the world. The latest print-on-demand technology ensures that the books will remain available indefinitely, and that orders for single or multiple copies can quickly be supplied.

The Cambridge Library Collection will bring back to life books of enduring scholarly value (including out-of-copyright works originally issued by other publishers) across a wide range of disciplines in the humanities and social sciences and in science and technology.

Hellenistic Military & Naval Developments

WILLIAM WOODTHORPE TARN

CAMBRIDGE
UNIVERSITY PRESS

CAMBRIDGE UNIVERSITY PRESS

Cambridge, New York, Melbourne, Madrid, Cape Town, Singapore,
São Paolo, Delhi, Dubai, Tokyo

Published in the United States of America by Cambridge University Press, New York

www.cambridge.org
Information on this title: www.cambridge.org/9781108013406

© in this compilation Cambridge University Press 2010

This edition first published 1930
This digitally printed version 2010

ISBN 978-1-108-01340-6 Paperback

HELLENISTIC
MILITARY & NAVAL
DEVELOPMENTS

Cambridge University Press
Fetter Lane, London

New York
Bombay, Calcutta, Madras
Toronto
Macmillan

Tokyo
Maruzen Company, Ltd.

Hellenistic Military & Naval Developments

BY

W. W. TARN

M.A., F.B.A.

CAMBRIDGE

At the University Press

1930

PRINTED IN GREAT BRITAIN

PREFACE

THE three lectures here published are the Lees-Knowles Lectures in Military History for 1929–30, delivered at Trinity College, Cambridge, in the spring of this year; they were somewhat shortened in actual delivery. The two matters which may perhaps claim some novelty, the evolution of the great war-horse and of the Hellenistic great ships, are now rather more fully treated, chiefly by means of notes and appendices; indeed, the principal justification for the appearance of these lectures in book form must be the section on the ships, about which comparatively little has hitherto been written to much purpose. Professor F. E. Adcock very kindly read through my typescript before it went to the publishers and made several suggestions, more particularly in the early part of the first lecture, which have much improved the book. My best thanks are due to him, and also to the Syndics of the Cambridge University Press for undertaking the publication of these lectures.

W. W. TARN

CONTENTS

Lecture I

GENERAL OUTLINE & INFANTRY

MY subject is the development of warfare[1] in the Hellenistic period, that is, roughly speaking, in Greece and Asia between Alexander and Augustus; I am not dealing with Rome. I shall take first the general outline of the subject and the history of infantry; the second lecture will deal with the use of animals in war, that is, cavalry and elephants, for this was essentially the age of cavalry; the third lecture must be given to machines, that is, siege warfare and naval warfare. I am afraid that in this lecture I shall only be treating well-known things, but I hope afterwards to have a little that is new both about horses and about ships. It may be an unfortunate thing that war should have occupied such a large place in the outlook

---

[1] The latest text-book is J. Kromayer and G. Veith, *Heerwesen und Kriegführung der Griechen und Römer*, 1928, which gives the literature of the subject. Accounts of most of the battles referred to can be found in the *Cambridge Ancient History*.

of every State during the period I am considering, but if we are going to try and understand the ancient world we cannot leave out any part of it. Some indeed believe that for the Graeco-Roman world war was at first, speaking generally, the normal condition and peace the abnormal one, and it is not difficult to find facts to support this, such as treaties of peace made for a short and definite term of years.

The warfare of the little states of classical Greece had once been a kind of seasonal occupation; the harvest was reaped early, and there was little to do for the rest of the summer: there were not many amusements, so you fought somebody. This phase was assisted by the shortage of agricultural land in Greece; even a few farms made a difference, and there was a constant temptation to start early and reap your enemy's harvest. Even in the third century this phase can still be detected in the constitution of one rather backward State, Aetolia. The Assembly met twice a year, before and after the campaigning season; at the first meeting they decided how they would spend the summer, and at the second, held in September, they stored the year's booty; this assumed that there would be

[2]

booty to store, that is, that they would have fought with or raided somebody. It seems probable that in this kind of warfare the loss of life was not, to our idea, proportionate to the amount of fighting, and indeed it has been defended on the ground that it operated as a useful natural selection; in hand-to-hand warfare the best men usually survived, and the reverse selection exercised by modern war was uncommon, unless the front-rank men got killed when a defeated force fled. Natural selection however was not really necessary, for the custom of rearing certain children only gave all the selection required; putting aside men maimed or blinded, I believe that in the whole of Greek and Macedonian history there is only one case—Alexander's cousin Harpalus—of a man being described as unfit for military service[1].

From this kind of warfare sprang the warfare of classical Greece. Normally, a battle meant that two lines of hoplites, well-armoured men

---

[1] The ἀδύνατοι at Athens who got the dole had to be τὸ σῶμα πεπηρωμένοι, though not necessarily through war, and unable to work at a trade, Arist. *Ath. Pol.* 49, l. 25. The ἀδύνατος in Lysias walks with two sticks; he of Aeschines, *Or.* 1, 40, ll. 30–40 is blind. This is hardly what we mean by "unfit."

with shield and spear, drawn up eight deep, met face to face and pushed. The square was known in the fifth century as a defensive formation, but otherwise there were really no tactics to speak of, and very strange it is when one considers how competent the Athenians were in naval warfare. Reserves were unknown; if anybody's flank ever got turned it was usually by accident, by the tendency of a line of hoplites to incline to the right so as to avoid exposing the unshielded right side, or by the men at the end of the line giving way, as happened when the Athenians outflanked and surrounded the Thespians at Delium. The use of the ambush was of course practised; Demosthenes in his campaign in Acarnania did once, by means of an ambush, turn his opponent's flank, and Brasidas at Amphipolis did in much the same way take Cleon in flank when his force was on the march; but I believe no case of an open attempt to turn the flank of the enemy in a battle is known. This may have been due partly to the fact that cavalry was hardly a serious force anywhere in Greece except in Thessaly, and Thessaly by language, history and customs belongs rather with Macedonia than with Greece, and will be noticed in the next lecture. All it came to, in most cities, was that a few wealthy men rode on horses; they were useful for scouting or raiding supplies, but they rarely played any serious part in battle; there is no case of Greek cavalry in Greece, putting Thessaly aside, either employing shock tactics or turning the enemy's flank. Certainly the cavalry of Syracuse was a more efficient arm; in 415 B.C. they saved the beaten Syracusans from the Athenian pursuit, and they were able to play a considerable part in compelling the Athenians to surrender in their final retreat from Syracuse; but Sicily was not Greece, and the pursuit of worn-out men was not a battle.

Much the same applies to the history of light-armed troops, who had to wait for Alexander to show what could be done with them. There *were* light-armed troops, usually armed with javelins, and a great city like Athens would possess some archers; but prior to the fourth century it seems that the light-armed were often only an un-organised force, and it was very rare for them to exert any serious influence on the course of a battle, except in Aetolia. That unconquerable country was always a law to itself; but, apart from the defeat of Demosthenes by its light-

[5]

armed levies in 426, the success of light-armed troops, in very unusual circumstances, against the Spartans marooned on Sphacteria is about the only exception of importance which occurs to me; for again the services of the Syracusan light-armed against the Athenians during their retreat from Syracuse had little to do with the use of such troops in battle. The bow in particular was not really a factor in Greek warfare, except in Crete, which lay rather outside the general stream of Greek history; the bow belongs to Asia, and will have to be considered together with cavalry. There seems to have been no case before Philip, unless Dionysius of Syracuse, of a general who really understood how to use a combination of various arms. But there was one development in armament before Philip, the invention of the peltast. The peltast, so called from his *pelta* or small round shield, was a lighter edition of the hoplite—smaller shield, lighter spear, less armour, greater freedom of movement; the later text-books treat peltasts as an intermediate arm between heavy and light infantry. They were known in the late fifth century, but they first became famous in the fourth century, when the Athenian Iphicrates and the

[6]

peltasts he had trained wore down and destroyed a small body of heavy-armed Spartans. But their importance really belongs to the rise of mercenary service.

Naturally there were generals who within their limitations were abler than their fellows, but perhaps the only one besides Xenophon who was of much importance for the *history* of land warfare was the Theban Epaminondas; Philip knew him, and he has been claimed as Philip's forerunner. He did not indeed rise beyond the idea of two lines of heavy-armed spearmen meeting face to face, but by increasing the number of files of his left wing—he made it a column 50 deep—he made sure of breaking the opposing wing of the enemy and then taking the centre in flank. He chose the left wing, not the right, partly because there was no fear of the left wing edging away from the enemy line to save their unshielded side, and partly because at Leuctra the Spartiates themselves were on the right of their army. His deep column won a famous victory at Leuctra over the Spartans, but it had in fact been used by Thebans before him, and once the device was known it was tolerably easy to meet. The two real novelties at Leuctra were that Epaminondas used the Boeotian cavalry, who were rather better than the cavalry of the ordinary Greek state, to guard the flank of his striking wing, and that he deliberately refused his weak right wing; both these things were an anticipation of later Macedonian tactics. But his early death prevented the ideas he had used at Leuctra from being further developed.

Most classical fighting was amateur fighting; men left their occupations to fight in the summer, and there was little temptation to study the art of war. Xenophon did study it, and his city never made use of him at all; Epaminondas won a great victory and subsequently served in the ranks. Men who regarded war in this light, however good fighters they might be—and they were good fighters—could hardly hope to make head against the Macedonians when they came. There was one city in Greece where every one from youth upwards was trained for war and war only; but the only advantages which Spartan *methods* possessed over those of their neighbours were that their graded corps of officers made them handier in manœuvre and that they might sometimes possess a more or less permanent general in one of their kings. Certainly pro-

fessionalism began early among men of Greek
blood, though on lines which had little to do
with the city state, but it seems to have originated with the Ionians of Asia; the Saïte kings of
Egypt in the seventh and sixth centuries had
Ionian mercenaries. Mercenaries recruited from
old Greece, largely from Arcadia, appear before
the end of the sixth century, and in the fifth are
found in the service of many tyrants, notably
in Sicily, as well as of the satrap Pissuthnes
(*Thuc.* III, 34) and probably of the Great King;
but these were men definitely recruited, and it
cannot be said that as yet there was a professional
class. That class seems to have really started with
the collection of adventurers and rough cha-
racters who in 401 B.C. followed the younger
Cyrus to the field of Cunaxa and were left to
fight their way home through mountain tribes
as best they could. In such circumstances the
ablest men, like Xenophon, came to the top
and got some real training; unfamiliar ways of
fighting, and the pressure of necessity, stimu-
lated invention; the use of the square received
a considerable impetus, and Xenophon had to
study rearguard fighting, and ultimately got the
idea of a sort of reserve. The remains of his

10,000 turned professionals when they reached the Troad, and from them dates the growth in Greek history of a world separate from the city state, the world of mercenaries, recruited from young men in the more backward districts, like Arcadia, Aetolia and Achaea, and above all from the exiles whom the wars of the fourth century in Greece manufactured in ever increasing numbers. Such men found leaders, like the Athenian Chabrias, who might be an Athenian general and fight for his country but might equally well fight for someone else, for instance Tachos, King of Egypt; and mercenaries who served such leaders became in a sense their men, like the bands of *condottieri* in the Middle Ages. Mercenaries were not more efficient than other troops, but they did familiarise men with the idea of war as a business and also with the idea of permanent commanders. For a time, too, they brought about one curious change. Whatever the reason—expense may only have been *one* factor—by Alexander's time the majority of mercenaries were probably armed as peltasts; this led to peltasts being sometimes put in the line—undoubtedly they were by the Persians at Issus—and for this they were not really fitted.

In the latter part of the fourth century came the great Macedonians—Philip, Alexander, the generals whom Alexander trained; and in their hands the whole idea of warfare was revolutionised, one manifestation of a new spirit which they brought with them. A Macedonian army was not, like a Greek army, a force of heavy-armed spearmen, but a balanced combination of a number of arms, each with its particular use. The most important section of it was the cavalry, and the greatest novelty was the sudden emergence of cavalry as the real striking force. Where Philip got the idea from does not seem to be known, but in Alexander's hands it was given such prominence that for a century cavalry was the all-important arm in Hellenistic warfare. As to the infantry, Alexander employed five sorts; two heavy-armed, the phalanx and the hypaspists; two light-armed, who used the javelin and the bow respectively; and his Greek mercenaries, who were largely peltasts; but his mercenaries need not be considered, as he used them mainly for subordinate work, that is, for garrisoning conquered territory and maintaining his communications.

The national weapon both of old Greece and

Macedonia was the spear, and neither people ever took very kindly to any other; the sword, for example, plays a very minor part in Hellenistic fighting, and the history of the sword belongs to the west, to the Celts, to Spain, to Rome. Most of Alexander's army used the spear in some form or other. But though the national Macedonian arm was the heavy-armed spearman of the phalanx, it was not till a much later time that the phalanx took first place in the Macedonian armies as we know them; that place was taken by the cavalry. The chief difference in Alexander's time between the Greek hoplite and the Macedonian phalangite was that the latter had a smaller shield and probably a longer though lighter spear. The phalanx was organised in battalions on a territorial basis; it was recruited from the Macedonian peasantry, and every free man was under obligation to serve; but as Alexander kept his men with the colours year after year till they became a professional force, and as it was also necessary to have the land cultivated, there must have been some system of not calling up all the members of a family, though during the great wars much of the cultivation was doubtless done by the women. As the file-leader in Alexander's phalanx was called *decadarches*, leader of ten (Arr. VII, 23, 3), the phalanx must once have been ten men deep, but under Alexander the usual depth was sixteen men, and this was maintained. The pretended retreats successfully made by Philip at Chaeronea and by Alexander at Massaga show the degree of training attained by this force; for to attempt a pretended retreat with imperfectly trained troops is very likely to end in a real one. Alexander was much concerned to keep the phalanx as flexible as possible; indeed, before he died he had a scheme to replace the middle ranks, who chiefly supplied weight, by archers and light-armed troops; but apparently it was never actually used, though a tactical writer seems to refer to it[1]. But even Alexander's phalanx had two disadvantages, which were to become accentuated later. The first was the difficulty of keeping line. To present to the enemy an unbroken row of spearheads was one thing; to present a row of spearheads with a gap in it somewhere was quite another; and when we come to consider the cavalry we shall see the enormous importance of that question of a gap.

[1] Asclepiodotus, 6.

In both of the big battles, Issus and Gaugamela, the battalions of the phalanx failed to keep line, and in each battle the real threat to Alexander arose from that fact. The one battle in which this difficulty was scientifically met was Pyrrhus' victory over the Romans at Heraclea; there Pyrrhus deliberately left gaps between the battalions of his phalanx and filled them with his Samnite and Lucanian allies, who fought in the same flexible maniple formation as the Romans and were thus able to keep the line between the several battalions. The second disadvantage of the phalanx was the apparent impossibility of forming front to the flank with any degree of speed. The flank of the phalanx was always extremely vulnerable, and had to be guarded with the utmost care. Alexander himself had no trouble, because he always took sufficient forethought; in a pitched battle he always guarded the unshielded side himself with the Companion cavalry. At Heraclea Pyrrhus had the flanks guarded by elephants as well as cavalry.

The length of the spear used by the phalanx, the *sarissa*, is a well-known difficulty. That the spears of the later phalanx were all of the same length and 21 feet long is tolerably certain;

apparently even longer spears were experimented with. But Theophrastus' statement that the longest *sarissae* in Alexander's phalanx were 12 cubits[1], generally assumed to mean 18 feet, is quite irreconcilable with the fact that Alexander often picked phalangites for forced marches and that these same *sarissae* were also used by some of his cavalry; unless we are going to suppose that the length of the spears in the different ranks varied greatly, for which there is no evidence. The solution, I think, must be sought in discarding the assumption that Theophrastus here means Attic cubits—cubits, that is, of 18 inches. There is a parallel in the length of Demetrius' battering rams, which Diodorus, after Hieronymus, gives as 120 cubits. The latest writer on siege-machines, Colonel E. Schramm, is quite clear that a ram of 180 feet would buckle, and suggests that cubits is a mistake for feet both here and in another passage he quotes[2]. But I think the simple explanation both of Schramm's difficulty and of the passage in Theophrastus is that we are dealing with a shorter cubit, probably Macedonian. The

---

[1] Theophrastus, *Hist. Plant.* III, 12, 2.
[2] In Kromayer and Veith, *op. cit.* pp. 235–7.

enormous difference between weights and measures of the same name in different places is notorious; and as the Macedonian stade—the stade of the bematists—was roughly only three-quarters of the Attic stade, and as the different stades in use in the Greek world were all based upon different lengths of the foot measure, there must have been a short foot in Macedonia to correspond to the bematists' stade and presumably therefore a short cubit also[1]. This would make Alexander's *sarissae* somewhat about 13 feet, which is much more probable.

The hypaspists, who after Alexander became a regular force in every Macedonian army and in all the Macedonian kingdoms, were also heavy infantry, and if there was any difference in armament between them and the phalanx it is not known what it was. A common view is that they were peltasts, but this is not supported

---

[1] The passage in Theophrastus is from the chapter on the cornel tree, and he gives as one of his two sources "some" who wrote of this tree as it existed in Macedonia. This must be the well-informed Macedonian source he uses elsewhere, *e.g.* at great length for the manufacture of pitch; the comparison with the *sarissa* was therefore made, as one would expect, not by Theophrastus himself but by someone in Macedonia who might naturally be expected to use Macedonian measures.

by any evidence, and it is quite certain, from the use made of them in many battles, that they were not[1]. It is not even probable that their armament was lighter than that of the phalanx; for on at least two occasions when Alexander wanted a small body of spearmen for a forced march, he picked the men, not from the hypaspists, but from the phalanx. In the wars of the Successors Alexander's hypaspists kept together as a corps—they appear under the name of Argyraspids, Silver Shields—and in the battles in which they took part they acted as the phalanx or part of it; while Perseus' hypaspists at Pydna are actually referred to as a phalanx[2]. The real distinction between the hypaspists and the phalanx was probably one of standing and recruitment; it was the difference between the Guards and the infantry of the line.

The great change in the nature of warfare is seen by the fact that the Macedonian heavy

---

[1] Their *shield* may have resembled the pelta, since Livy calls them *cetrati*, XLIII, 41.

[2] Livy, *ib.*, where *leucaspidem phalangem* is the hypaspists or cetrati; see Ed. Meyer, "Die Schlacht von Pydna," *Berlin. S.B.* 1909, pp. 794–8, who however retranslates cetrati by Peltasten, though he *means* hypaspists, see p. 793, "die Peltasten oder Hypaspisten, lat. cetrati."

infantry, corresponding to the old Greek spear-line, played a comparatively small direct part in the conquest of Asia, though of course it played a large part indirectly, for it will be seen in the next lecture how important it was even to the best cavalry to have a background of perfectly steady infantry. In some of the battles of the Successors infantry seems to have been even less of a factor; for example, at the battle of Parai-takene between Antigonus and Eumenes of Cardia, Eumenes' phalanx, completely victorious as against that of Antigonus, was brought to a dead stop by Antigonus' cavalry, and at the battle of the Dardanelles between Craterus and Eumenes Craterus' Macedonian phalanx sur-rendered without a blow after its cavalry had been defeated. In only two of Alexander's battles, apparently, did the phalanx play much direct part; one was Issus, where Darius had some 12,000 Greek mercenaries, and the failure of the phalanx to keep line in crossing the river let the Greeks in, with results which might have been serious had not Alexander's right been able to take them in flank; the other was the battle outside Massaga, where Alexander led the phalanx himself. In the hardest fight his infantry had, the battle with Porus' elephants, he only used two battalions of the phalanx. It is the more noteworthy that in his two principal forced marches—the pursuit of Darius and the rush from the Jaxartes to relieve Maracanda— he took a number of phalangites with him as well as cavalry, in spite of the slower pace this entailed. In the pursuit of Darius this is understandable, for he may not have trusted the information he received that Darius' Greek mercenaries had left him; but the reason for his action in the march to Maracanda is lost. Evidently he was very loath to trust to cavalry alone, whatever the emergency.

I think no one can read Arrian without realising that the greatest share in the conquest of Asia, after the cavalry, belonged to the light-armed troops. No important State before Alexander, in the Greek-speaking world, had taken the use of light-armed troops in battle really seriously; their business had been scouting or pursuit, and they were essentially the arm of the more backward States. Even after Alexander, though many forms of light-armed troops were found in Hellenistic armies, we seldom hear of their doing anything particular in battle; the

[19]   2-2

principal exception is the action of Eumenes II, who must have studied Alexander very carefully, when at Magnesia he used his light-armed to break up the charge of the scythed chariots in the same manner as Alexander had done at Gaugamela; these troops were thrown right forward to shoot down horses and drivers or pull them down with their hands, tactics which (though it is not expressly recorded) may have been based on the fact that scythed chariots required room to work up their full speed and were easier to handle if met soon after starting[1]. Of the three weapons of light-armed troops, the bow, the javelin, and the sling, two had their real home in other lands; the bow and the javelin essentially belong to Asia. The sling, though brought to perfection only (it seems) in the Balearic Islands, was widespread as a weapon; the Rhodian slingers, of whom Athens enlisted 700 for the Syracusan expedition, had a reputation which they upheld in Xenophon's retreat and were perhaps the first of the Aegean peoples to use leaden bullets[2]; but though Philip II had

[1] Plutarch, *Sulla*, 18. Cf. the charge in Xenophon, *Cyrop.* VII, 1, 29.
[2] G. Fougères, *Glans* in Daremberg-Saglio.

employed slingers with heavy stones in the
siege of Olynthus¹, the very trifling use made of
slingers by Alexander shows that he only considered them useful for irregular work, and the
knowledge of what the sling could really do in
expert hands was reserved for the armies of
Carthage and Rome.

But the bow and the javelin, though Asiatic,
were at home also in two countries within Alexander's sphere, the javelin in Thrace and the
Balkans, the bow in Crete, and Alexander took
advantage of this to include both weapons in his
army; he had a body of Cretan archers and bodies
of Thracian and Agrianian javelin-men. The
Thracians only played a subordinate part, but
the Agrianians and Cretans were in the thick of
every action, and Alexander's estimate of their
merits is shown by the fact that on the voyage
down the Jhelum he took them on shipboard
with him like his own Guards, while the rest of
the army had to march. These two corps together, among other things, met and broke up
the charge of the scythed chariots at Gaugamela,
decided the battle with the nomads on the

¹ D. M. Robinson, *Amer. Journ. Arch.* xxxiii, 1929,
p. 76.

Jaxartes, fought against Porus' elephants, and were meant to be the mainstay of one of the two converging attacks, which never took place, on the first day at Aornos. It was not in human nature that there should not be rivalry between the two, and this rivalry furnished an incident of some interest. The Agrianians are never recorded to have failed in anything they were given to do, but the Cretans failed once; in the fight in the Balkan pass on the way to the Danube, where the tribesmen hurled down wagons on the advancing army, the Cretans were driven back while the Agrianians stood their ground. Alexander remembered; and years afterwards, at the Jaxartes, he personally led the Cretans alone across the river in advance of the army to keep a space for the rest to land behind them; that is, he gave them the opportunity to get their own back. I suppose things like that were among the reasons why his army worshipped him.

In his use of light-armed Alexander was developing a new form of warfare; no doubt it was part of the general principle which led him wherever possible to avoid the waste of mere hammer-and-tongs fighting by using his brains.

But it seems to have been a line of warfare which underwent no further development after his death, though if we had Seleucid history we might conceivably be able to add something as regards the employment of light-armed in mountain warfare. Otherwise, infantry, so long as the Hellenistic kingdoms lasted, was to remain very much as Alexander left it, with two exceptions: there was a later development of the phalanx, and there was an enormously increased employment of mercenaries. He only used Greek mercenaries in subordinate positions, and his army was essentially a national army; but in the long wars of the Successors after his death the generals used anything they could get, and much of the infantry employed was mercenaries, not merely Greeks, but drawn from every sort of people— Thrace and Asia Minor were favourite recruiting grounds—and sometimes armed in the Macedonian way. This rather altered men's ideas of warfare. So long as war was a national matter, as it had been for the Greek states and always was for Macedonia itself, men might fight as they do fight when national feeling is involved; but wars largely fought by mercenaries in the service of generals who had no national basis behind them

[23]

called out no feeling amongst the mercenaries. They were often true to their oath, though they could sometimes be bribed; they fought well enough so long as it was worth fighting; but there was nothing in particular to *die* for, and if their own paymaster was killed or thoroughly defeated they made no difficulty about surrendering and entering the service of the victor. Consequently for a time, until settled kingdoms again formed, a type of warfare prevailed in which the object was, not to destroy the enemy —nobody wanted to destroy useful mercenaries —but to compel him to surrender and then enlist him yourself; and sometimes this desirable result was achieved by bribery and propaganda without fighting at all. There were exceptions, of course; the little band of half-starved mercenaries who followed Demetrius to the end in his last war with Seleucus were frankly heroes; but some of the battles in the wars of the Successors did not involve a great deal of killing, and as those wars lasted off and on for forty years it was perhaps just as well.

This type of warfare left its mark on all the three Macedonian kingdoms which ultimately formed; all largely employed mercenaries to

spare their national armies. Macedonia of course
had a true national army, and the Ptolemies and
Seleucids did what they could to create one by
means of military settlements; they settled men,
not only Greeks and Macedonians, but Thracians
and Asiatics, on allotments of land, farms, which
they held on condition of coming up for service
if required; they thus had a stake in the country
and formed a sort of quasi-national nucleus of
the army, and in Asia at any rate the military
settlers had a genuine feeling of loyalty to the
Seleucid dynasty. But the system which had
obtained under Alexander and his immediate
successors, when large bodies of Macedonians
remained permanently on service and became
long-service professional troops, was dropped;
it was impossible to maintain it, for it was drain-
ing and ruining Macedonia. Instead, the standing force of the kings, if they kept one, was composed of mercenaries, who were willing to serve
professionally for a number of years with the
implied condition that they were given a farm
at the end; and the national army in all the
kingdoms—that is, the peasantry in Macedonia
and the military settlers elsewhere—went back
to what it had been in Macedonia before Philip,

a levy of men whose real business was farming and who were only called out in some really important crisis; for less urgent matters mercenaries were used, and the national troops were always spared as much as possible. A good illustration of this is the retreat of Philip V through Aetolia in the War of the Allies, after he had sacked Thermum; the country was difficult and he expected a surprise attack, so on the retreat he had his Macedonians guarded on all sides by troops whom he could better afford to lose.

Before coming to general questions I had better finish the history of the phalanx. During the century after Alexander, when cavalry was the dominant arm, there was little temptation to over-specialise, and the phalanx was fairly successful even when it met the Roman legions. One can hardly quote Xanthippus' defeat of Regulus, for though the Carthaginian phalanx fought well the battle was largely won by the elephants and the overwhelming Carthaginian cavalry; but at Heraclea Pyrrhus' phalanx defeated the legions in a battle of sheer hammering, though at a great price. Over-specialisation came in when the reign of cavalry ended. Several

[26]

reasons contributed to end that reign. One was the accident that, at the battle of Raphia in 217 between Antiochus III and Ptolemy IV, the two wings cancelled out and the battle was finally decided by the heavy infantry of the centre. Another was the fact that Hannibal, whose cavalry was excellent, had ultimately been unable to conquer the Romans, whose cavalry was inferior. But probably the main reason was the action of Macedonia. After 279 B.C. the Antigonid kings ceased to be interested in Asia, and the battles they fought on land were either with Sparta or some other Greek state, or with their neighbours, Epeirots and Dardanians. All these peoples sooner or later adopted the Macedonian phalanx and its weapons; none were really strong in cavalry; Sparta in particular continued to fight as she had always fought. Consequently the Antigonid kings neglected their cavalry and forgot Alexander's lessons; while Alexander had 5000 or even 7000 horse to a phalanx of 12,000, Philip V at Cynoscephalae had only 2000 horse to a phalanx of 16,000. The Antigonids returned to pitched battles of heavy infantry, and as their Macedonians could always win such battles they gave their whole attention to the phalanx. By the second century it had become cumbrous; the spears had become 21 feet long so as to get five spearheads projecting before each file of men, and now required both hands to use them; and a form of close order known as over-shielding came into use, each man being covered by the shield of the man on his right, and the files being so close together that they could only go straight ahead. The new phalanx offered certain recruiting advantages, for it could be worked if only the first five rows and the rearmost were composed of trained men, while the other rows were filled up with half-trained men who just pushed; and, face to face, it was a terrible engine of destruction. But even the comparative flexibility of Alexander's phalanx had been lost, and rough or hilly ground always disordered its too rigid formation.

Consequently when Macedonia met Rome the splendid Macedonian infantry was largely thrown away. While the phalanx had become more dependent than ever on somebody guarding its flanks, both cavalry and flank guards had been neglected, because in fighting Sparta these things did not matter. Against the legions they did matter, vitally, for the legions were a very flexible formation and able to take advantage of circumstances, while the phalanx could not. Given its own conditions—a formal battle on level ground, with an Alexander or a Pyrrhus to guard its flanks—the later phalanx would have defeated the legions or anything else; but a formation which can only fight under special conditions has ceased to be of much use. The later phalanx fought four battles against Rome: Cynoscephalae, Pydna, Magnesia, Corinth. It failed at Magnesia because Eumenes of Pergamum rolled up Antiochus' horse from the flank and so came in on the flank of the phalanx. It failed in the battle between the Achaeans and Romans at Corinth because the superior Roman cavalry took it in flank. At Cynoscephalae the battle started in an affair of outposts on hilly ground, and Philip was forced against his judgment to support his men; the right wing of the phalanx carried all before it, but the left was defeated as it came up and before it ever got into formation, and twenty maniples then took the right wing in rear. Its best chance was at Pydna. Here the flanks were not assailed and may therefore have been sufficiently guarded; but, like Philip at Cynoscephalae, Perseus attacked when he was not really ready, to support his skirmishers, and though at first the phalanx swept everything before it, bad timing allowed an undefended gap in the spear-line to open between phalanx and hypaspists; some Roman troops thrust into the gap, and that was the end. The phalanx lingered on for a time in Asia—Mithridates of Pontus used it—but with the fall of Macedonia and Achaea its effective military history was ended.

I come now to more general questions, and the first is the functions of the commander. In a Greek army before Alexander the general made his arrangements before action, and in action merely led his men. The modern idea of a general not fighting himself but keeping behind the line and directing operations never seems to have occurred to anyone; and obviously it was a difficult thing for anyone to start, partly because his enemies in the city would have accused him of cowardice and partly because, in simple warfare, the moral effect of the commander giving a lead was very great. Moreover, if a battle merely consisted of two lines of spearmen meeting face to face, the moral effect was a much greater factor than brains behind the line could be. In consequence, reserves were unknown.

I mentioned that Xenophon once employed reserves; but these were not true reserves, that is, a body of men under the general's own hand to be used by him as circumstances might dictate; Xenophon merely posted two small bodies of men behind the line with orders to reinforce any point that seemed likely to give way, and as the battle in question was broken off soon after it started, no opportunity was given for seeing how his plan would work. Alexander maintained the old custom and always charged at the head of his cavalry; he enjoyed himself so thoroughly that he probably never thought of doing anything else. But, being Alexander, he never charged till he was certain that he could produce a decisive effect. At Granicus, where he had a considerable superiority in numbers, he charged instantly, and the battle was practically over before the rest of his army had crossed the river. At Issus he waited till his light-armed troops had driven off the Persian light-armed who were threatening his flank. But at Gaugamela he waited quite a long time, and the battle on the flank there is very important for the general's functions.

As Alexander was outnumbered, more particularly in cavalry, he formed his army as three sides of a square, with provision for completing the square if required; he himself with the Companion cavalry was at the right-hand end of the front, so that he was also the pivot of the right-hand side of the square, or rather the flanking column, extending backwards behind him. Facing him was the Persian cavalry of their left wing under Bessus, satrap of Bactria. The battle opened on this side with Bessus sending a body of Saca horse to ride round Alexander's flank and attack the flanking column. Alexander ordered one of the formations of the flanking column to meet them; and he and Bessus alternately fed in fresh troops till the whole of his flanking column was in and the whole of Bessus' cavalry; then, and not till then, Alexander, having seen that his men could hold Bessus without him, made the charge with the Companions which broke the Persian line. This battle on the flank at Gaugamela, compared to an ordinary Greek battle, is like the transition from ancient to modern times; Alexander has the whole of the flanking column under his hand and moves them as the occasion demands. But Bessus was doing much the same thing with his cavalry, and Bessus is nowhere represented as a man of outstanding ability; consequently the idea of the commander of a *wing* having control over his troops and using them according to the course of the battle can hardly have been a new discovery. Instances of such action can indeed be found in an earlier period of the fourth century, though very much less elaborate than the tactics of Alexander and Bessus at Gaugamela; examples are the pretended retreat of Philip at Chaeronea, and the action of Pelopidas in his battle with Alexander of Pherae, where, though he himself led the hoplites, he was nevertheless able to recall his victorious cavalry from pursuit and turn them against the enemy centre[1].

Now if we compare Gaugamela with the battle of Carrhae in the first century we see at once that something has happened in the interval; for while at Gaugamela Alexander retained control over one wing of his army, at Carrhae the Parthian general Surenas has the whole of his army under his control from beginning to end and manœuvres it as he pleases to suit the circumstances. Indeed, the change can be detected much earlier; at Mantinea in 207 B.C. Philopoemen had

[1] Plutarch, *Pelop.* 32.

sufficient control to make some alteration in his dispositions and win a victory after his left wing had been driven off the field. I know no case in Hellenistic history of a general being outside the battle altogether in the modern sense; but clearly a movement was at work which made for less participation in fighting by the general and greater control. This movement is sometimes supposed to have originated with Hannibal, but it can be traced much further back. I rather think the crucial battle is Paraitakene, fought between the two best generals of Alexander's school, the elder Antigonus and Eumenes of Cardia.

Leaving out non-essential matters, the arrangement of both armies at Paraitakene was two long lines of infantry with cavalry on either wing. But all the cavalry had its own commanders, and at the opening of the battle both Eumenes and Antigonus with their bodyguards were on the extreme outside of the cavalry of their right wings; Eumenes also had 300 picked horse in reserve behind him, the first true reserve known. Unlike Alexander at Gaugamela, Eumenes evidently knows throughout just how the *whole* battle is going, and can signal simple

movements by trumpet; Antigonus, though
equally well informed, apparently has to com-
municate with his men by mounted messengers.
But the point is this. Eumenes' right and centre
were victorious, and the advance of the heavy
infantry of the centre opened a gap in his line
between centre and left; Antigonus at once
seized his chance, rode through the gap—it is
implied that he did this himself—and took
Eumenes' left in flank—the inner flank. Now if
Antigonus had still been on his own extreme
right, where he started, he could not have done
this; I conclude that at the critical moment he,
with his bodyguard, was watching events from
behind the line of his right wing and was thus able
to seize his chance. The reason then why both
generals started at the extreme end of the line
was that they could subsequently take up any
position they pleased without disturbing the
line; this must have been known beforehand to
their men, so that there should be no question
of their men thinking they were running away
if they moved, as happened in the case of
Labienus at Munda. Paraitakene then furnishes
the first case known of a general directing the
whole battle. I expect that, if we had a proper

account of Ipsus, we should find Seleucus also directing his half of the battle from the rear; he was not with his cavalry on the wing, and he cannot have been in front of his phalanx; at the same time he knew what was happening to his cavalry, for it must have been he who gave the order so to dispose the elephants as to cut Demetrius off from the battle. The later battle of Chaeronea between Sulla and Archelaus furnishes a close parallel to Paraitakene in the freedom of movement enjoyed by both generals and the amount of control they exercise, though, as at Paraitakene, both still fight themselves.

A point of importance here is the leadership of the phalanx. When a king led his phalanx in person, how did he do it? He certainly did not send away his horse and take somebody's spear. There was no room for him inside the formation. And if his phalanx was meeting another phalanx he could not ride at its head, for that was certain death when the two lines met. Now in the second phase of the battle of Mantinea Philopoemen advanced with his phalanx, but he was at the side of it, on the side which had been uncovered; and when Antigonus Doson commanded his phalanx at Sellasia, or Ptolemy IV the Egyptian phalanx in the second phase at Raphia, they may have been in the same position. In any case they were outside the ensuing battle with the enemy phalanx.

I have gone rather at length into this question of the functions of the general, because it is perhaps the most important single matter in the history of ancient warfare. I do not think that in our period we can go further than this: the general did not altogether cease to fight, but he obtained control of the battle, and the way was being prepared for the idea of the general as director only.

Rome apart, the dominant tactics of this age were so essentially cavalry tactics that I must postpone considering them till the next lecture; but certain principles of war and of strategy require notice. For with Alexander and his generals we seem to pass from ancient to modern war. Consider for example what is called the first principle of offensive strategy, to seek out and destroy the main force of the enemy. Doubtless this had always been known; but Greek warfare, except for Epaminondas, had too often merely meant expending energy on the capture of unimportant places, which brought no decision. Contrast an instance of the grasp of first principles recently revealed through a Babylonian astronomical table[1]. It was in Antigonus' last war, in 302 B.C., when Lysimachus was invading Asia Minor and Seleucus was advancing from Babylon to join him. Antigonus, with much of his army in Europe, had no troops to stop Seleucus; but he sent a detachment to occupy Babylon behind Seleucus' back on the chance of making him turn to save his capital. Had he done so, Antigonus would have won his campaign in Asia Minor and Seleucus would have been crushed afterwards. But Seleucus let his capital go, joined Lysimachus, and recovered Babylon and much else by defeating Antigonus' main army. The same grasp of principle can be traced throughout the history of the Antigonid kings; it is interesting to follow it out in Doson's campaigns which ended with Sellasia, and even in the actions of Philip V in the War of the Allies, once it be understood what he was doing[2]. Or take the question of war on two or

---

[1] F. X. Kugler, *Sternkunde und Sterndienst in Babel*, II, pp. 438 *sqq.*; see Tarn, *Class. Rev.* XL, 1926, p. 13.
[2] I have tried to explain this, *Cambridge Ancient History*, VII, ch. 23, pp. 763 *sqq.*

more fronts against organised opponents. The first case in Greek history, I believe, of war on two fronts in the modern sense happened two years after Alexander's death, when Perdiccas in Asia, who then claimed to be Regent, was faced by war with Antipater and Craterus coming from Europe and with their ally Ptolemy in Egypt. Perdiccas had neither precedents nor text-books to guide him, nothing but his own grasp of first principles; but he seems to have adopted without the least hesitation the plan which is now commonplace knowledge, that you must attack on one front and stand on the defensive on the other. All the main principles of the war on two and on three fronts, and the use of interior lines, can be found illustrated at length in the two great wars waged by the first Antigonus against the coalition of dynasts who surrounded him.

As regards the methods of warfare Alexander introduced a number of things which were new, and the only question is if they held their ground in the later period. For instance, he discovered the principle of "March divided fight united," but I do not recall ever meeting this again prior to Antony's disaster in Armenia. He was not actually the first to press the pursuit of a beaten enemy so that he should not re-form, for it is now known that Philip had done this in his wars in the Balkans[1], but he was the first to do it after a great battle; the pursuit after Gaugamela was continued for 56 miles. Probably no such pursuit actually took place again in our period, but the principle was not forgotten. Another thing was the enormous speed of his forced marches, which remained a permanent acquisition in field warfare. It had once seemed a great thing that a small Athenian force should move quickly from Athens to Marathon and back again; but when Alexander chased Darius for 400 miles at a speed which his historians believed to have averaged 36 miles a day, excluding two or three rest days, or when he did 135 miles to relieve Maracanda in a little over 72 consecutive hours[2],

[1] See U. Wilcken, *Berlin. S.B.* 1929, p. 298, n. 6.
[2] Some modern parallels are given by Riepl, *Das Nachrichtwesen des Altertums*, 1913, pp. 135–6 (I am indebted to Dr M. Cary for this reference), who decides that 45–50 miles in one day is possible for an army; this covers Alexander's marches. I doubt if, when *all* the circumstances, especially the great heat and the perpetual fighting, are taken into account, either Alexander or anyone else equalled Havelock's march to relieve Cawnpore.

a new thing appeared in the world. Men's ideas of what an army could do were permanently modified, as appears from many instances: Antigonus' surprise march from Cappadocia to Pisidia, Demetrius' raid on Babylon from Syria, above all the feat of Philip V in reaching Sparta via the Gulf of Ambracia on the fourteenth day after quitting Thermum in Aetolia, which no one believed possible till he appeared.

In fact Alexander taught the West that in warfare distance was no longer a prohibitive factor. He maintained his communications throughout; at one time they stretched from Macedonia to the Punjab, and his most advanced base, Taxila, was still linked up with the homeland. Others were able to copy; both Seleucus and Antiochus III, in various campaigns, must have maintained very long communications. Two of Alexander's pupils performed peculiar feats in the matter of advanced bases. In the winter of 302 B.C. Lysimachus' advanced base at Heraclea on the Black Sea was cut off from his own kingdom, but nevertheless he won his campaign next year; while in 318 B.C. Eumenes, under pressure of necessity, abandoned his

Mediterranean bases altogether, advanced into Asia, and based himself afresh upon Persis.

But one other matter which Alexander introduced did not last, the habit of fighting in winter. Greek citizen armies, with other occupations, had naturally not done this; if occasionally a siege was continued through the winter, as at Potidaea, there was a sense of hardship. With Alexander, military exigencies overrode other considerations; the year he was pressing forward to reach Bactria he never took winter quarters at all, and he always attacked hill tribes in winter if he could, because the snow then kept them down in the valleys. He rested his men on other principles, according to the work in hand; in Sogdiana he rested them in the autumn before his winter campaign in the hills. His pupils sometimes continued the practice, if necessary; the actual decision in the war between Antigonus and Eumenes fell in a very cold January. But even in the generation of the Successors war largely came back to being an affair of the seasons, and so it remained. One reason was because so many campaigns included naval operations, which were impossible in winter; another was connected with the uni-

versal employment of mercenaries. For in the
third century mercenaries were engaged, not by
the year, but by the military year, which seems
to have varied between nine and ten months;
that is, the world of mercenaries had succeeded
in establishing a rule that they should have a
holiday in winter. When Hieronymus of Cardia
wrote his history of the two generations after
Alexander he dated by campaign years, just as
Thucydides had done. Nobody could have
dated Alexander's history by campaign years.

I mentioned at the beginning of this lecture
that the Macedonians revolutionised warfare.
The great change they made was not this or that
technical improvement, or even better generalship; it was the infusion of a new spirit. When
Alexander after Gaugamela took steps to prevent his enemy ever fighting again as an
organised force, he was doing exactly what
Nelson afterwards meant when he said that a
victory was not complete if one ship of the line
got away. This new spirit is not quite expressed
as a change from the amateur to the professional,
though that is in a sense true; it is not merely
that, with the necessary qualifications, we almost
feel as if we had passed from the ancient to the

modern world, though that in a sense is also true. It was rather the intense earnestness and thoroughness which they brought to bear on the matter. They had no precedents, but they understood principles; if you had to fight, you fought for all you were worth, and with every sort of weapon, except one. They did *not*, as a rule, practise the things we call atrocities; on balance, Macedonian warfare was distinctly more humane than either Greek or Roman; for example, for exactly a century after Alexander's death no city, so far as is known, was destroyed in war, a matter upon which Polybius commented after the bad old custom had come back again[1]. The one exception is Philip V in his middle period, when he was trying Roman methods of warfare. But if unorthodox weapons helped you, if it aided your military operations to start a revolution, to employ propaganda (propaganda is not an invention of the twentieth century), to create a combination reaching from Epirus to India, you just did these things as part of the day's work. When somebody put to Antigonus Gonatas the question beloved of later text-book writers: "How should one attack the

[1] Polybius, XVIII, 3, 4–8.

enemy?" his answer was, "Any way that seems useful[1]."

I should like to give one or two instances of what I mean, and I will leave Alexander out of it. Take the battle of Byzantium. The position was that Antigonus, on the Asiatic side of the Dardanelles, wanted to wrest the control of the sea from Polyperchon, the then regent in Macedonia, who had most of the Imperial fleet; Antigonus had 130 ships only. His fleet engaged that of Polyperchon in the Bosphorus and was decisively beaten, only some 70 ships escaping. By all the rules of war the matter was settled; what did happen was that twelve hours later Antigonus was sole master of the sea. He guessed, or discovered, that the victorious admiral, thinking it was all over, would go ashore on the European side for the night. He got part of his army across in the dark with boats, crowded his 70 beaten ships with good troops, and at daybreak caught the sleeping victors between two fires and captured their whole fleet. But had not Lysander done something of the sort at

[1] Stobaeus, *Flor.* IV, 13, 46, ed. Wachsmuth: ἢ δόλῳ ἠὲ βίῃ ἢ ἀμφαδὸν ἠὲ κρυφηδόν—a combination of bits of two separate lines of Homer, *Od.* 9, 406 and 14, 330.

Aegospotami? Yes, but he had not done it the night after a crushing defeat.—Or take Cassander's return to Macedonia. He was besieging Tegea; meanwhile the whole of Macedonia had gone over to Olympias, who was supported by King Aeacides of Epirus, Polyperchon and his mercenaries, and the Aetolians; and the Aetolians had cut Cassander off by occupying Thermopylae. It was an almost impossible position; it might have seemed that the only thing open to him was to attempt to fight his way back and die like a hero. What he did do was to cut down some trees and build rafts, which no one had thought of before; he floated his army on these rafts past the Aetolians into Thessaly, raised a revolution in Epirus which disposed of Aeacides, and bribed Polyperchon's mercenaries to desert him; Olympias' own folly did the rest. Not very heroic, perhaps; but most amazingly efficient.

I could multiply instances; but the contrast to most of the warfare of the centuries before Alexander is sufficiently obvious, always excepting naval warfare. After Alexander, beside that very great man Eumenes of Cardia, a Greek here and there learnt Macedonian ways; like Pythagoras.

Pythagoras was a revolutionary, a general of Nabis of Sparta; and when a very large and victorious Roman and allied army attacked Sparta and forced their way in, Pythagoras drove them out again by setting fire to that quarter of the city[1], a feat which deserves to be remembered. But, as a rule, even the most competent Greeks, good fighters as they were, continued to fight in the old way. Take for example the Athenian Leosthenes, who commanded the Greeks in the Lamian War. He was a capable general; early in the war he defeated Antipater and shut him up in Lamia. He had only a limited time in which to take the city, because reinforcements for Antipater were coming from Asia; he had plenty of men, timber on the hills, skilled artisans and money in Athens; and he had himself witnessed Alexander's methods. Yet he never attempted to make siege engines and storm the city; he blockaded it as though the world were still young, and that lost the war.

My last illustration shall be to compare the best Greek of the third century in the military

---

[1] Fire had been used before; but firing your own city was a very different thing to (say) Nicias' fire in Thucydides, VI, 102.

sense, Cleomenes III of Sparta, with a Macedonian king whom historians call incompetent and who lived a century later in a period called decadent, Demetrius II of Syria. It never occurred to Cleomenes, in his struggle with Antigonus Doson of Macedonia, that the Dardanians on Macedonia's northern frontier were always ready to invade that country; so they invaded it of themselves a fortnight *after* he fell, when he might so easily have hastened them and saved himself. Demetrius wanted to recover Babylonia from Mithridates I of Parthia, and it did occur to him that it would be useful if the Bactrians attacked Mithridates in rear. There was no apparent means of communicating with Bactria, as the Parthians held every known route, only he did it; his envoy must have gone right through Parthia disguised as a trader. The Bactrian diversion called off Mithridates and enabled Demetrius to recover Babylonia, though he was not strong enough to hold it.

I have given a brief outline of some of the principal changes which took place in warfare, and I should like to end with a moral tag, as one used to do in the Victorian period. It is this, that it may always be worth while studying

Macedonian warfare, not for the sake of warfare, but just for the sake of seeing the distinction, in difficult circumstances, between the man
who, as we say, does his best, and the man who
means to get the thing done and does it.

Lecture II

CAVALRY AND ELEPHANTS

IN the first lecture I considered the general
features of Hellenistic warfare, and more
especially the infantry; it is now necessary to
consider the development of cavalry. The history
of cavalry at this time belongs primarily to Asia,
just as the history of infantry belongs to Europe;
but the cavalry arm had been well developed in
two Greek-speaking countries, Macedonia and
Thessaly, and it was really the conjunction of
Asiatic horse with Macedonian leadership which
for a century after Alexander made cavalry the
dominant arm. This was followed by a period in
which such preponderance did not exist; then
a new set of circumstances brought about a revival in Asia, and the period we are examining
closes with a cavalry victory more extraordinary
than anything Alexander ever dreamt of.
Closely bound up with the history of cavalry is
the history of the bow, a weapon whose for-
tunes were largely omitted from the first lecture.

CAVALRY & ELEPHANTS

When the Persians[1] overran Western Asia
they won their battles by a combination of
cavalry and the bow; their archers threw the
enemy into disorder, and then the cavalry
charged and finished up what the archers had
begun. It has recently been suggested that the
spear, rather than the bow, was the national
weapon of the Persians[2]; but even if Darius I
does speak metaphorically of the triumphs of
the Persian spear, and pictures of Persian spearmen exist, I feel little doubt from the course of
history that the traditional view is the correct
one. The Persian cavalry consisted of the retainers of the barons and landowners, who under
the Persian land system lived each in his castle,
ruling his estate, which was cultivated for him
by the serf population of the villages; his retainers were not a paid force, but he fed them
and mounted them and they fought for him. It
was very much the same system as obtained
among the landowners on both sides of the
Border in the old Border wars between England
and Scotland; with the necessary allowances,

---

[1] On Persian arms and tactics see, besides Delbrück,
W. W. How, *J.H.S.* XLIII, 1923, p. 117.
[2] A. S. F. Gow, *J.H.S.* XLVIII, 1928, p. 133.

the castle of a Persian noble probably bore a
considerable resemblance to Scott's Branksome
Hall. When the Great King went to war he
called out his barons and gentlemen, who came
with their mounted retainers; this gave him an
efficient cavalry force. But, except for his own
professional foot guards and the Persian archers,
he had no good infantry; he had only half-
armed serfs or undisciplined hill tribesmen; that
is why Persian infantry, except the archers, was
a negligible force. The Persian archers do not
fit into the land system as we know it, and have
never been explained; possibly Persis itself was
not a country of serfs but had a free peasantry
belonging to the ruling race, like Macedonia,
and this peasantry supplied the archers.

In Greece the Persians met a new kind of
infantry, the Greek hoplite, who was a heavily-
armoured spearman; at both Marathon and
Plataea he showed that he could charge through
arrows successfully, and at Plataea he showed
also that he could, for a time, stand and be shot
at without becoming demoralised. Consequently
the Persian tactics failed; at Marathon they had
no cavalry, but at Plataea their cavalry was successfully countered, for one of the Greek flanks

rested on a wall and one on the mountains, and neither could be turned. Indeed, at Plataea the traditional Persian tactics doubly failed; the Greeks were not thrown into disorder by the arrows, and between this fact and the protection of their flanks the cavalry were unable to charge them with any effect. Mardonius did charge when the day was lost, and got killed; probably it was deliberate, for he did the thing which cavalry never could do; he charged an unbroken spear-line. So far as is known, there is no case of this ever having been successfully done.

Plataea definitely killed the Persian archer as the main Persian infantry force; at Cunaxa the bow played little part, and in the Alexander story archers are only mentioned at Issus, where they were quite a subordinate arm. If they could not hold off the spearmen they were useless; once at close quarters, an unarmoured man with a dagger had no chance against an armoured man with a spear. But very few in Greece, I imagine, ever supposed that the Persian cavalry had failed; what had beaten *them* was the hill-ground. This comes out very clearly in Xenophon. The Persian cavalry at Cunaxa, though not numerous, did two things; they won the battle, in spite of the Greek hoplites, and they also charged right through a force of peltasts, who were light spearmen; this narrowed the inability of cavalry down to this, that they could not charge an unbroken line of heavy-armed spearmen. There is little to learn from the retreat of the Ten Thousand, because they were never seriously attacked by any Persian force; but one most important incident for the history of cavalry took place in Xenophon's battle with the Bithynians. When the Bithynians were put to flight the satrap Pharnabazus interposed his cavalry to cover their retreat, and the Greeks made no attempt to pursue because (I quote Xenophon's words[1]) "the cavalry made them afraid." Pharnabazus' cavalry cannot have been numerous, and the Greeks were over 6000 hard-bitten men; this is the first instance in classical times of that moral dominance which from Alexander onwards cavalry were to exercise over infantry. Certainly Agesilaus was not afraid of Tissaphernes' horse; but then he had cavalry himself, and also, if the long but broken account in *Hellenica Oxyrhynchia* VI is to be trusted, he defeated Tissaphernes at Sardes by means of an

---

[1] *Anab.* VI, 5, 29.

ambush[1]. The Persian cavalry in the fifth century had apparently been armed with three weapons—short spears, bows *or* javelins, and daggers[2]; but when Alexander invaded Asia it seems to have been armed only with javelins and daggers, the leaders alone, the aristocracy, having scimitars. Xenophon had known of horses wearing some form of protectivè covering (see *post*) and does once mention a small force of mounted archers[3]; but mounted archers, so far as I know, never appear in Persian armies in the Alexander story, and indeed it looks as if by his time the bow had ceased to play much part in Persian warfare.

I turn now to the cavalry of Europe, which for our purpose means Thessaly and Macedonia; leaving Sicily aside, Greece proper has but little cavalry history, though two states, Argos and Boeotia, did manage to do something with cavalry and could raise enough to give Alexander a small contingent. Certainly in the early second century the cavalry of the Aetolian

---

[1] Xenophon makes it a straightforward attack, *Hell.* III, 4, 23 = *Agesilaos*, I, 31, but his account is very brief.
[2] Herod. IX, 84 + 61; X, 49.
[3] *Anab.* III, 3, 7 and 10.

League was much praised; but as the League then included part of Thessaly the League cavalry was probably largely Thessalian, as the cavalry of Pelopidas had been in his battle with Alexander of Pherae. It is unfortunate that we know so little of the Thessalian cavalry, which had a long history; as early as 511 B.C. 1000 Thessalian horse in Hippias' service had defeated a small body of Spartan hoplites under Anchimolius, and in 455 the Thessalian cavalry had foiled an Athenian invasion. Thessaly in the fourth century was still largely a country of great landowners ruling a serf population, the Penestae; its land system therefore approximated to the Persian type, and it may be that the Thessalian cavalry was recruited in the same way, that is, that it consisted of landowners and their retainers and had little to do with the towns. This might explain why the Thessalian cavalry apparently had certain traditions of its own, as though it were a definite body and not a collection of little units from various cities. A late writer, Philostratus, gives a picturesque account, which ought to be true, of a military display given by Alexander's Thessalian horse when he visited the tomb of Achilles at Troy; it ended with the horsemen galloping round the tomb at full speed and calling on the names, not only of Achilles, but of his famous horses Xanthos and Balios[1]. Poseidonius' pupil Asclepiodotus, who wrote a pedantic book on tactics, has a circumstantial story (VII, 2) that the Thessalian cavalry, unlike others, was accustomed to manœuvre in the formation of a diamond, with one angle toward the enemy; it seems such an unlikely thing for anyone to invent that it may represent some old tradition. Alexander treated his Thessalian horse as the equal of the Macedonian, and the Thessalians were the mainstay of the Greek forces in the Lamian War; it was through his victory over their cavalry that Polyperchon, who afterwards became regent in Macedonia, acquired his considerable military reputation.

The Macedonian cavalry had quite a different history, which must go back to the very cradle of the Macedonian people; they represented the king's original retinue, who had ridden with him in battle when Macedonia was a monarchy of the heroic type. Under Alexander the place of the original retinue had been taken by his

[1] On this story see G. Radet, *Notes critiques sur l'histoire d'Alexandre*, vol. I, 1925, pp. 5, 12.

Companions, a body of men of high rank, about 100 in number; but his principal cavalry force, the Companion cavalry, still showed its descent both by its name and by its composition, for it was composed of aristocrats and landowners, though as it was now recruited on a territorial basis it probably included some wealthy men from the towns. The Companion cavalry, which was at one time 2000 strong, was the force which Alexander usually led himself and was till after Gaugamela the most important formation in his army; the only other Macedonian cavalry he ever used was a small body of lancers, doubtless recruited from the people, and they are not heard of after Gaugamela; much of his cavalry was drawn from subjects or allies, at first the Thessalians, Greeks, Paeonians, and Thracians, and later the peoples of Eastern Iran and the steppes. With his death the nature of the Macedonian cavalry changed, and his Successors must have recruited their Macedonian cavalry from among the people; this or that general might call some regiment his Companions, but the real Companion cavalry hardly outlived Alexander. It could not from its nature be filled up by recruiting, though at the end he enrolled a few noble Persians; before he invaded India its numbers were so reduced that he broke it up and made new cavalry formations, hipparchies, each containing only one squadron formed from the Companion cavalry and being filled up with Asiatic horse. At the end of his life he again collected what remained of the Companion cavalry into one hipparchy; but after his death every Macedonian aristocrat became of importance, and the Companions dissolved into the "Friends" who gathered round the leading satraps; that was the end of probably the finest cavalry force the ancient world ever saw.

It is remarkable how few in number the cavalry were who revolutionised all existing notions of warfare. The expedition of Cyrus the younger had shown that for successful warfare in Asia cavalry was needed on a scale quite different from anything Greece had yet dreamt of; but Alexander's force, though adequate for complete success, was anything but large. He began with a little over 5000 horse; at Gaugamela he perhaps had 7000; he had slightly over 7000 in India, of which some 6000 were Asiatics. If he found this enough, as he did, it is clear that the cavalry forces which he met were not really large, either. The figures relating to Persia in the Alexander-historians are generally worthless; but I have tried, for my own information, to deduce the *possible* total of cavalry in the Persian Empire under Darius III from indications given by Hieronymus, and the conclusion, for what it may be worth, is that about 45,000 to 50,000 would be an outside figure[1]. Of course there was nothing in the least approaching this in action at Gaugamela; Alexander was heavily outnumbered, but there is a very definite limit to the extent of that outnumbering, especially if the excellence of some of the Asiatic horse be considered. In the great battle of Ipsus, with the whole world in arms from the Adriatic to the Indus, the total cavalry engaged on both sides, including Macedonian, Thracian, and mercenary horse, was under 21,000.

When there is a disparity of strength, the balance has to be redressed by generalship and tactics. But Alexander's cavalry tactics were very much those of the Persians; all along the two sides learnt from each other. Doubtless the Companions were really a better force than any 2000 men of the enemy, but we cannot say more

[1] See Appendix I.

than that; in their desperate battle with the Persian Guard in the last phase of Gaugamela the Persians broke through them, not away from them. Alexander's advantage really lay in two things: his own unique faculty for seeing the right moment to do the right thing, and the steadiness of his background, the Macedonian infantry, with which the Persians had nothing to compare. His actual tactics varied in every battle, as did those of the Persians also; but already under his Successors tactics were beginning to crystallise, and with the third century they became and remained stereotyped; the third Antiochus fought Magnesia very much as the first Antigonus fought Ipsus, and lost it for the same reason. It is worth considering tactics in some detail.

Given a strong cavalry force, there were three uses you could make of it. You could merely fight with the enemy's cavalry; or you could take his infantry in flank or rear; or you could break through his line. Alexander used all three methods, but merely to defeat the enemy cavalry was clearly to him the least important, and it was unfortunate that this became later the regular object of Hellenistic warfare. I gave in my first lecture a few instances of how competent the warfare of the Successors was; but, except Antigonus, they did not handle their cavalry as Alexander had done, and it was doubtless this which led to tactics becoming stereotyped, until the Parthians struck out an entirely new line. Except for Paraitakene, the one battle in Asia in which a cavalry leader showed Alexander's spirit was the action of Eumenes II at Magnesia; and there he, like Alexander, had the advantage of a perfectly steady background, the Roman legions.

I will take first the matter of breaking the enemy's line. I have mentioned that there was one thing cavalry could not do, charge an un-broken spear-line; and I have also noticed the difficulty heavy infantry had in maintaining their line unbroken. Now if you will imagine your-self seated on a horse and watching an advancing line of spear-points, and if something happens to that line whereby the spear-points vanish from one bit of it, leaving a gap, you will realise that that gap must draw you irresistibly to it; that is the point you will certainly ride for. Over and over again, in Hellenistic literature, we get allusions to that gap; and that was the chance for cavalry to break the line. The first recorded case, I think, in classical history is Cunaxa, which was won by Tissaphernes throwing his cavalry into the gap caused by the Greek advance[1]; and the last case I know of is Paraitakene, where the victorious advance of Eumenes' right and centre opened a gap between his centre and left into which Antigonus threw his cavalry, threatening to cut off and destroy Eumenes' left. It did not win the battle, for Eumenes' men were too steady; but it stopped Eumenes' advance dead, and compelled him to bring back his line to the aid of the threatened left wing.

In between these two battles comes Gaugamela, which is the classical instance of cavalry breaking the line. It was always Macedonian custom to have the heavy infantry in line, with the cavalry on the two flanks, a custom which lasted as long as the Macedonian States. But this was not the Persian custom; though they usually had their infantry in line with cavalry on either flank, they generally had a cavalry force in the middle of the line also, and as that was the king's position, this force included the Persian

[1] See my reconstruction of Cunaxa, *Cambridge Ancient History*, VI, p. 8.

[63]

Guard, a picked body of 1000 men. But at
Gaugamela the Persians had no genuine infantry
line at all; they knew their infantry was of little
use, so the line was a mixed one of infantry and
cavalry, with two very powerful cavalry wings;
if they were going to win, they had to win with
their wings. I alluded in my first lecture to the
cavalry fight on the one flank between Alexander and Bessus, in which Alexander had the
better; a similar fight took place on the other
flank between Parmenion's cavalry and Mazaeus,
in which Parmenion was so hard pressed that
two battalions of the phalanx had to support
him. The consequence of this fighting on the
wings was that when the two lines advanced
both failed to keep line. The Persian line
stretched out to help Bessus and opened a gap;
Alexander at once charged the gap with the
Companions and broke the line. But his phalanx
in advancing also opened a gap, for two of the
battalions were involved with Mazaeus' cavalry;
the Persian cavalry of the Guard, followed by
other horse, at once charged that gap and cut
the phalanx in half. But though the two charges
were very similar, the effect produced was very
different; for, while the Persian line broke, the

Macedonian line did not, which illustrates once
more the advantage to a cavalry general of trustworthy infantry behind him. The Persian Guard,
after riding through the phalanx, neglected the
first principles of war and made for the baggage,
when they ought to have taken the phalanx in
rear. I once wrote that they were out of hand[1];
but I think now that in reality they were acting
on a mistaken sense of loyalty, for Darius'
family were with the baggage and they wanted
to rescue them. But the way to rescue them was
to defeat Alexander.

There was one battle in which a stationary
line was broken by cavalry, and therefore no
question of a gap arises: Alexander's charge at
Issus. Opposed to him were the Persian archers,
and behind them the Persian troops called
Cardaces. The Cardaces are supposed to represent an attempt made by the Persians to form a
professional infantry, but even if this be the case
nobody knows how they were armed; conceivably they were peltasts, and the Persian
horse at Cunaxa had already ridden through
peltasts. But even if they were hoplites, there
was no question of Alexander charging an

[1] *Cambridge Ancient History*, VI, p. 382.

unbroken spear-line, for he drove the archers back upon them and this must have thrown them into confusion.

I come to the second thing you could do with a cavalry force: take the enemy infantry in flank or in rear. Alexander perhaps did this after breaking the line at Issus, though it is more probable that the troops which took the Greeks in flank were the hypaspists; but in Macedonian warfare after his death it seems as if everyone was alive to the risk and as if the defence was usually adequate; for whatever happened in the cavalry fighting on the wings we never hear of cavalry getting in on the flank or rear until Eumenes II at Magnesia defeated the cavalry of Antiochus' left wing and proceeded to roll up his army from the flank. It was, however, successfully done by the cavalry of Carthage in battles against Romans, by generals who understood the lessons of Macedonian warfare; while Scipio finally learnt from Carthage how to use his cavalry at Zama. When the Spartan Xanthippus defeated Regulus, the Carthaginian cavalry got in on both flanks; but the most perfect instance was Hannibal's use of his heavy cavalry at Cannae. Alexander had always had an

offensive and a defensive cavalry wing, Parmenion with the Thessalians forming the defensive wing while he attacked with the Companions. One of his best pupils, Eumenes of
Cardia, had used either an offensive and defensive wing (as at Paraitakene) or two offensive
wings (as in the Dardanelles battle) as circumstances dictated; but by Hannibal's time, judging from the account of Raphia, Macedonians
had forgotten the use of a defensive wing.
Hannibal at Cannae returned to Alexander's
way; he had his heavy cavalry under Hasdrubal
on his left, while on his right his light Numidian
horse formed a defensive wing, whose business
was merely to keep the Roman cavalry on that
side occupied. Hasdrubal completely defeated
the Roman cavalry on his side, rode round the
rear of the Roman army, defeated the cavalry on
the other side and left pursuit to the Numidians,
and then rode back once more and took the
Roman infantry in rear. I suppose that is the
high-water mark of cavalry achievement in the
first cavalry period. Alexander at Gaugamela
had the Companions so well in hand that after
breaking the Persian line he was able to turn
them and ride back; Hasdrubal at Cannae

turned his victorious cavalry *twice*. It was Hasdrubal's exploit which called forth the sentence in which Polybius (III, 117, 5) sums up the century during which cavalry was king of the battlefield: it is better, he says, to have only half the enemy's infantry and a preponderance in cavalry than to be equal to him in both arms.

Several Hellenistic battles merely exhibit a cavalry fight on the wings which led to nothing but a useless pursuit of the defeated force; a good instance is Raphia, where both the right wings chased both the left wings off the field and the decision was left to a parallel encounter between the heavy infantry of the two centres, a wasteful business. Another case is the successful charge of Antiochus III at Magnesia, which lost the battle. The classical example is Demetrius' pursuit of Seleucus' cavalry at Ipsus; one has read many comments on how Demetrius lost his empire by losing his head, but I do not feel too certain about this. We have to explain the peculiar fact that Seleucus was not leading his own cavalry; it may be that he thought he could exercise the functions of a general better elsewhere, but it may also be that he laid a deliberate trap. His cavalry—light horse from Eastern

Iran—was perhaps meant to run away, so as to give the elephants the opportunity of cutting Demetrius off from the rest of his army; in that case Demetrius, with the enemy cavalry not really broken, had a more than usually difficult decision to make. For it was difficult in any case, apart from the possibility of your own men getting out of hand, to know exactly when to break off pursuit of the beaten cavalry; if you pursued too far the battle might be lost behind your back, while if you checked pursuit too soon and fell on the enemy infantry the beaten cavalry might rally and take you in flank. It was the intuitive knowledge of the proper moment to stop which marked the great cavalry leader. But many Hellenistic generals, right down to Magnesia, made matters worse for themselves by following the custom of charging with the cavalry at the opening of the battle. Alexander seldom did this; at Issus, and still more notably at Gaugamela, he delayed his charge till it could be made with quite decisive effect; this was one of the things which distinguished him as a cavalry leader from his imitators.

It remains to notice one or two battles in which the defeat of the enemy cavalry was itself the end aimed at. Such a battle was Alexander's first victory, at Granicus; he saw that the Persians on the river bank were a smaller force than his own, and that what infantry they had was out of action behind their cavalry, and he therefore charged at once with the cavalry of his right wing; there was not much for his centre and left to do by the time they had crossed. But the type of this battle was dictated, not by Alexander, but by the Persians. The Persian leaders had the first rule of war clearly in sight—to destroy the main force of the enemy; but as they had not nearly enough men to defeat the Macedonian army, they decided to risk everything on striking at the brains and will of that army, that is, on trying to kill Alexander himself, which would have ended the war. The extraordinary formation they adopted was to induce Alexander himself to charge, and their concentrated attack on his person only failed of success by a fraction of a second. The other battle in which Alexander was solely concerned with the enemy cavalry was that with Porus' elephants, which I shall come to later; but one of Eumenes' battles must be noticed here, that against Craterus at the Dardanelles. Craterus had a vast superiority in the quality of his 20,000 infantry, but his Macedonian horse were outnumbered by Eumenes' Cappadocians. Eumenes, as his only chance, attacked at once on both wings and was victorious on both, whereon Craterus' infantry surrendered.

This battle exhibits that moral domination of cavalry over infantry which was one of Alexander's legacies; it had been shown the moment he died, when in the quarrel between infantry and cavalry it was the infantry who shrank from trying conclusions; it was shown again very notably in Peithon's campaign against the revolted Greeks in Bactria. The Greeks had 20,000 foot and 3000 horse, all veterans. Perdiccas could easily have given Peithon greater numbers, but in fact he gave him only a small infantry force; for he had 8000 Asiatic horse, and both generals regarded this as decisive, as it was. A mere demonstration of his cavalry strength sufficed to make the Greeks surrender without fighting, though it is fair to add that treachery was also at work.

The weapon of Alexander's cavalry, except the lancers, was the *xyston*, the short cavalry spear. At Granicus and Issus the Persian horse used javelins and daggers; subsequently each

side borrowed from the other. Before Gaugamela part of the Persian horse was re-armed
with spears, and after it Alexander raised a body
of horse armed with javelins. All through the
Macedonian period these two, the short spear
and the javelin, were the standard cavalry weapons; various modifications were tried, like the
distinction between javelin-men who had swords
and javelin-men, called Tarentines, who relied
on the javelin alone. Alexander in India experimented with horse-archers, and so occasionally did the Seleucids; but the horse-archer
apparently was of small importance. Beyond this
we get no innovations, down to the temporary
eclipse of cavalry in the second century B.C.; then
came the Parthians, and cavalry in Asia secured
a predominance greater than it had ever had
under the Persians or the Macedonians. The
Parthian re-organisation of Iran cannot be dated,
but doubtless it had some connection with the
great nomad invasion; it cannot be later than
the beginning of the first century B.C. All the
old formations and weapons were swept away;
infantry to all intents and purposes was given
up; and Iran adopted just two cavalry types, the
horse-archer and the heavily mailed lancer or

cataphract. Both must have their story told, and I will begin with the cataphract.

Cavalry could not charge the heavily-armed spearman. But if you put the heavily-armed spearman himself on a horse, armoured the horse also, and lengthened the spear, then cavalry could charge anything. That was the idea behind the cataphract cavalry, which developed from small beginnings till it came to differ only in one particular from the knights of the Middle Ages. Its origin, so far as is known, goes back to some of the nomad or semi-nomad peoples of Central Asia, the less developed members of the Iranian family. These peoples were principally horse-archers, but the aristocracy wore some kind of coat-of-mail (the Sarmatians began by making theirs of horse-hooves), put a breast-plate on their horses, and fought hand to hand. It was doubtless from the people of the steppes that the Persians got the idea of some form of protection for the horse, though I think it is only mentioned once: Xenophon records that the horses of Cyrus' bodyguard were protected in some form[1], and he was so struck by the idea that he not only transferred it to the

[1] They wore προστερνίδια and προμετωπίδια, *Anab.* I, 8, 7.

horses of the first Cyrus[1], but himself advocated its general adoption by cavalry[2]. But the Sacae-Massagetae had already evolved regular breast-plates of bronze for their horses before the time of Herodotus[3]; and the 1000 mailed Saca horse who fought for Darius III at Gaugamela were doubtless of this type. When the Parni from the steppes originated the Parthian monarchy, their aristocracy must have brought this mode of fighting with them; and we subsequently get the same development as in the Middle Ages, the armour becoming heavier and the spears longer. In the first century B.C. the Parthian cataphract or knight wore a helmet and a long coat of mail to the knee[4]; his legs below the knee were similarly armoured; his horse was encased in iron mail[5]; and his spear had grown so enormous that Greeks called it *kontos*, which means a barge-pole. He still often carried a bow, but his real weapon was his great spear. He is called an iron man, built into his armour[6]; and Tacitus

---

[1] *Cyrop.* VI, 1, 50-1; VII, 1, 2. [2] περὶ ἱππικῆς, XII, 8.
[3] I, 215, περὶ τὰ στέρνα χαλκέους θώρηκας περιβάλλουσι.
[4] Figures: Fr. Sarre, *Die Kunst des alten Persien*, Pl. LXV; Fr. Cumont, *Fouilles de Doura-Europos* (1922–23), Pl. XCIX, 1. [5] Suidas *s.v.* θώραξ.
[6] Suidas *loc. cit.*; Plutarch, *Luc.* 28.

(*Hist.* 1, 79) says that the Sarmatian cataphracts were rather helpless if knocked off their horses, just like the mediaeval knights. The chief difference was, that whereas the mediaeval knight was armoured all over, the cataphract had no thigh armour under his coat, I suppose because he was riding without stirrups and grip was all-important; it may have been this which led to the invention of stirrups[1]. Now on horseback the coat of mail would pull up, leaving a vulner-

[1] Stirrups were unknown to Greeks, Romans, Parthians, and also to the Scythians (E. H. Minns, *Scythians and Greeks*, p. 75). Professor Rostovtzeff says that the first ones occur in the Sarmatian graves of the Kuban country, *Iranians and Greeks in South Russia*, p. 130, cf. p. 121; these graves are, generally speaking, of the first century B.C. to the first century A.D. (pp. 128, 139). Stirrups also occur in the early Iron Age in Siberia, among a Hunnic people (Minns, *op. cit.* pp. 250, 277, 279). Mr S. W. Bushell (*Chinese Art*, 2nd ed. 1910, vol. I, p. 27) says that the riders on the Shantung bas-reliefs of the first century B.C. have stirrups; the objects in question might in themselves be only leg coverings, but certainly the riders have not the attitude of men riding without stirrups. Some Chinese stirrups are also figured by Rostovtzeff, *The Animal Style in South Russia and China*, 1929, Pl. XXIII, 4; query, Han period (p. 107). It may therefore be doubtful whether the actual inventors were the Sarmatians, the Huns, or the Chinese; though they are things which two peoples might well invent independently.

able spot above the knee; and Roman tacticians used to advise taking the cataphract sideways and striking at that bare spot[1].

Antiochus III made the acquaintance of the cataphract, such as he then was, when he invaded Parthia, and he experimented with some at the battle of Magnesia; they did no good, for Eumenes took them in flank. As Lucullus also had little trouble in outmanœuvring the Armenian cataphracts, the West may have thought at first that here was only another case of over-specialisation, such as had killed the phalanx. But the cataphract was saved by his mobility, and I suppose his effective use was largely a matter of generalship; he had a longer innings than the mediaeval knight, for there was no gunpowder to interfere with him. For centuries cataphracts were the weapon of Asia; the Sassanians took them over from the Parthians and I believe made them their chief arm, and the Sarmatians, who probably developed independently of the Parthians, gave the Roman Empire much trouble.

Now if you desire to armour both the man and the horse, the extent to which you can go

[1] Plutarch, *Luc.* 28.

depends on the strength of the horse; and the horse of the steppes, though fairly strong, was not normally strong enough to carry armour and a heavily-armoured rider. No doubt the nomads did their best to develop some heavier horses; the Wusun, for instance, had a breed which was stronger than anything the Chinese knew of prior to the first century B.C.; but the same Chinese account also shows that the horses of the Wusun could not compete in strength with those of Parthia[1]. It is impossible to speak about the Parthian horses without recalling the memory of a great Cambridge scholar, the late Sir William Ridgeway. In his book *The Origin of the Thoroughbred Horse* Ridgeway put forward a theory of the origin of the great warhorses used by the knights of the Middle Ages. Now these great horses were developed not once, but twice, in history; Ridgeway did not consider the Parthian horses, and it seems to me possible—it will be understood that what follows is put forward rather in the nature of a

[1] I quote Ssu-ma Ch'ien, *Shi-ki*, ch. 123, throughout from the translation by Fr. Hirth in *Journ. American Oriental Soc.* XXXVII, 1917, p. 89. For the Wusun horses see p. 103.

suggestion—that they furnish a confirmation of his theory. That theory, so far as required for my present purpose, and put very briefly, was that the great mediaeval chargers were evolved from crossing the northern horse with Libyan blood, and that when we meet Libyan horses in Greek story they figure as divine, like the mares of Aeneas in the *Iliad*; Pegasus, for example, was a Libyan stallion. We shall meet Pegasus presently.

The basis of the great horse in Parthia was the Nesaean horses of Media[1], a huge herd which the Persian kings kept in a district in Media where grew the famous Median lucerne, the alfalfa. Herodotus (III, 106) calls them larger than others; but there is a seal in the British Museum which shows the first Darius driving a pair[2], and they are certainly not heavy horses. I imagine, from the dates, that it was the Seleucids who began to develop them and the Parthians carried on the work, for the great horses were already in evidence by 106 B.C.;

[1] Strabo, XI, 525, practically identifies the Nesaean horses of his own day with the Παρθικοί; for their great size see Philostratus, *post*. For the Chinese material here see Appendix II.

[2] Figured by Sarre, *op. cit*. Pl. LII, and by Ridgeway, *op. cit*. p. 193.

indeed it may be that the key to some of the obscure history of the early Parthian kings is to be found in attempts to deprive the Seleucids of this herd. For Pliny (*N.H.* vi, 113) says that Parthia was bounded on the west by an otherwise unknown Median people called Pratitae; the word seems to represent the people of the *pratum* or meadow (doubtless it is a translation of some Iranian word), that is, the Nesaean fields, and Pliny's statement, which can only refer to some definite date before Mithridates I conquered Media, may relate to a time when the Seleucids were just keeping their enemies out. The final development of the great horse can be seen in the wonderful chargers of the Sassanian reliefs[1], so very like the pictures of the great German and Flemish warhorses of the Middle Ages, with enormous chests and barrels and strong necks, but much finer feet than the feet of a carthorse. These are the horses Strabo meant when he said that the Parthian horses "had a shape of their own[2]," and that Philostratus meant[3] when he said that the Indian elephant

---

[1] Sarre, *op. cit.* Pls. LXXI, LXXIII, LXXIV, LXXVIII, LXXIX, LXXXV.

[2] XI, 525, ἰδιόμορφοι.   [3] *Life of Apollonius*, II, 12, 54.

[79]

was as much bigger than the African elephant as was the African elephant than the Nesaean horse—a silly *cliché* as regards the elephants, but perfectly good evidence for the size of these horses in the second century A.D.

The great Nesaean horses, with the Median lucerne on which they fed, travelled to Ferghana, the country on the Jaxartes which was the last outpost of Hellenism in the north-east and which formed an independent state of some kind when the Graeco-Bactrian empire broke up; there the Chinese heard of them as being something much superior to the Wusun horses, which they already possessed, and as they were at this time learning from Iran to use the heavy outfit of the mailed horseman[1] they greatly desired those horses. The Emperor Wu-ti[2] sent an army in 106 B.C. which failed to reach Ferghana, and another in 101, which succeeded in getting a few of the horses, with a promise of some more; they are described as superior in strength to the Wusun horses and were (I quote Professor

---

[1] B. Laufer, *Chinese Clay Figures*, 1914, pp. 217 *sqq.* M. Rostovtzeff, *Mon. Piot*, XXVIII, 1925–6, p. 136; *The Animal Style in South Russia and China*, p. 107.

[2] This story is given at length by Ssu-ma Ch'ien (Hirth, pp. 109 *sqq.*).

Laufer[1]) distinguished by noble proportions and slenderness of feet as well as by the development of chest, neck and croup. Apparently the breed can be traced in Chinese art[2].

Now on Ridgeway's theory the great Nesaean horses should have been developed from the original Nesaeans through the introduction of Libyan blood, and where Libyan horses occur they are called divine; and the contemporary Chinese historian Ssu-ma Ch'ien does relate that the Ferghana horses were descended from a "heavenly horse" and that when brought to China they themselves were christened "heavenly horses[3]." If this stood alone, it would be difficult to avoid believing that this story of divine descent came to China with the horses and that the "heavenly horse" of the Chinese historian was a Libyan stallion. But in another place Ssu-ma Ch'ien has quite a different account[4]; a

---

[1] *Sino-Iranica*, p. 210.   [2] See Appendix II.

[3] Hirth, p. 95, § 18, and p. 103, § 79. The heavenly horse is called T'ien-ma, and the horses are said to "sweat blood." Hirth, p. 140, says that the term *han-huë*, "sweating blood," may really be a transcript of some foreign sound. Perhaps some Pahlavi scholar will explain it.

[4] E. Chavannes, *Les mémoires historiques de Se-ma Ts'ien*, vol. III, pp. 236–7.

"heavenly horse" had been seen and recognised in China, running wild, twenty years previously, and what Wu-ti got from Ferghana was a "heavenly horse" itself and not merely the descendants of one; a poem remains which he is said to have written to celebrate its arrival. There might then have been an independent Chinese legend about a heavenly horse[1]; but even if there was, this in itself would not suffice to account for the divinity of the Ferghana horses, because that divinity apparently occurs also in Iran, where it would hardly be derived from a Chinese legend. Seven years ago a clay seal was dug up at Susa which bore the figure of a winged horse, like Pegasus[2]. It is said to belong to the Sassanian period; but the horse itself, an attractive little figure, if not Greek work, is like a copy of Greek work, very much as similar Greek figures, Tritons, centaurs, and so on, appear in the art of India, and winged horses on the famous white bronze mirror of the Han period with Graeco-Bactrian

[1] According to Ssu-ma Ch'ien, Wu-ti found in the Book of Changes that "the divine horse will come from the north-west." (Hirth, p. 103.)
[2] J. de Morgan, *Rev. d'Assyriologie*, XX, 1923, p. 39.

designs[1]. Now this little horse, though winged
and flying, is an unmistakable representation of
one of the great chargers which are so well
known from the Sassanian reliefs; and I have
failed to see any connection between these
chargers and a figure of Pegasus except Ridgeway's theory. If then we accept that theory as
he worked it out for the chargers of the Middle
Ages, things seem to fall into place. The great
horses of the Parthian period are stated to be
descended from a heavenly horse, that is, on the
hypothesis, from a Libyan stallion; Pegasus
ought also to be a Libyan stallion; and on the
Susa seal we have a descendant of that divine
Libyan stallion portrayed as Pegasus. Of course
it may all be only a set of coincidences; but it
does seem to me more likely that we have here
a curious confirmation of Ridgeway's view.

The cataphract cavalry became the weapon of
Asia; but in the first century B.C. it looked as if
that weapon was going to be the other Parthian
formation, the horse-archer. All the steppe
peoples were horse-archers, and doubtless the
Parthians brought this arm with them from the

[1] In the Victoria and Albert Museum; see Bushell,
op. cit. Fig. 60.

steppes; but they were only a small body who took over the rule of a highly organised kingdom, and at first they used infantry like the Seleucids, and must also of course have used such cavalry as Iran could supply them with. But at some period before the first century B.C. they swept away all existing cavalry weapons and arranged that the nobility of their empire should equip their mounted retainers with the bow alone[1]; and much trouble was taken to teach these men to shoot. They seem also, judging by one most striking representation which has reached us, to have taken as much trouble over breeding light horses for the archers as over breeding heavy ones for the cataphracts[2]. This reliance upon horse-archers

[1] On the asymmetrical bow of the nomads used by Parthians, longer on one side of the grip than the other, see Minns, *op. cit.* pp. 61, 66.

[2] Compare the known figures of steppe horses—for example Pl. XXI in Rostovtzeff, *Iranians and Greeks* (see p. 109), and the terra-cotta of a Parthian or nomad horse-archer in Sarre, *op. cit.* Pl. LIV—with the beautiful Parthian horse on the reverse of Labienus' coin (G. F. Hill, *Historical Roman Coins*, No. 80), which has almost the look of a thoroughbred. See also a little bronze Parthian horse and rider in the British Museum, No. 117,760.

was probably one of the reasons why, prior to Carrhae, the Western world formed such wrong ideas about Parthia; for the West did not think much of horse-archers, and except in Crete had never taken very kindly to the bow. It was not really a Greek weapon[1], even if the archers of Athens or Megalopolis were sometimes useful; Homer himself is not too sure about the bow— poor creatures like Paris use it; a real gentleman, like Odysseus, leaves his bow at home when he goes to fight. In the Persian war the spear had beaten the bow, and even Persia had largely abandoned it; the use Alexander made of it in the hands of his Cretan archers does not seem to have found many imitators. Neither did it improve matters much, in Western eyes, if the archer was mounted. One of our losses is a proper account of the battle Alexander fought with the nomads across the Jaxartes; Arrian's story is unintelligible, except that somehow Alexander's light-armed played the decisive part. But when the nomads broke, Alexander pursued them for a very long way, which looks as if they had run out of arrows; certainly he was

[1] So, from a different angle, E. Kalinka, *Klio*, XXII, 1929, p. 250.

not much impressed by them. He enlisted 1000 horse-archers from the nomad Dahae for his Indian expedition, but they seem only to have done subordinate work, and the same thing was true of the armies of his Successors and of the Seleucids; they often possessed a small corps of mounted archers, Dahae or others, but these were only one of various small bodies who might be useful for a special purpose. There were some in Armenia, but Lucullus did not have much trouble with them. The explanation of all this must simply be a universal belief that they soon ran out of arrows and were then useless. This idea is found as early as Herodotus, in his description of the battle between Cyrus and the Massagetae: the two sides first shoot away their arrows at each other, apparently without doing much harm, and then come to close quarters and the real work begins; the description itself is pure fancy, but shows the belief. It is found again in Justin's statement (XLI, 2, 8) that Parthians could not fight for long; and even as late as Carrhae the Roman troops expected that the Parthian arrows would soon be exhausted, which means that that is what their officers had told them.

No doubt the reason why the Parthians took to horse-archers, apart from any question of hereditary instinct, must be connected in some way with the great nomad invasion of Parthia, the nomads being chiefly horse-archers; but in a sense it was the logical outcome of everything that had been happening since the battle of Plataea. The old Persian tactics had been a combination of foot-archers and cavalry, and had definitely failed at Plataea. No infantry system to replace the archers had been evolved in Asia; every king had used some European system, first the Greek mercenaries of the later Achaemenids, then the mercenaries of every nationality employed by Alexander's generals, then the Graeco-Macedonian settlers and mixed mercenaries employed by the Seleucids. But Graeco-Macedonian settlers were of little use to the Parthians, and though at first they used mercenaries, in 128 B.C. their mercenaries had turned against them; so they really returned to the old Persian system, cavalry and the bow, but modified to accord with the lessons of history. It had been shown that foot-archers could not break up heavy-armed infantry before that infantry charged them; by mounting the archers the

[87]

Parthians made it impossible for infantry to charge them, and so gave the bow a better chance. Of course the archer might still be attacked by cavalry, and to meet this they developed an old form of desert tactics which consisted in pretending to fly and shooting back over the crupper, the famous "Parthian shot"; Xenophon had seen it done[1], and it is shown on a fragment of a vase from South Russia representing nomads[2], so it was not a Parthian invention. Again, it had been demonstrated that unless something first disordered the spear-line cavalry could not charge it, and that archers could not be relied on to throw it into disorder; by armouring horse and man and producing the cataphract cavalry the Parthians acquired a force which could charge any troops and had not to wait for the archers to break them first[3]. As they could not get infantry of a good type, and as inferior infantry would only have been a handicap, they took the logical course, which the Achaemenids had never done, of relying upon cavalry

[1] *Anab.* III, 3, 10.
[2] Minns, *op. cit.* p. 55.
[3] Plutarch, *Ant.* 45, gives a case of cataphracts charging the legions even when in their closed formation.

alone and abandoning the use of infantry altogether; the cataphract horse could fulfil some of
its functions. Nevertheless, two difficulties still
remained. The cataphracts might charge anything, but at a price—a price paid by the nobility
and the most expensive horses; it was better if
some other way could be found of dealing with
heavy infantry. But that depended on the horse-
archer; and *he* ran out of arrows.

It was in these circumstances that the military
genius appeared who, in his brief life, up-
set all previous ideas of warfare and made the
horse-archer the potential master of the world.
We do not know his name; we only know his
family name, Surenas, general of King Orodes
of Parthia, the man who defeated Crassus. It
occurred to him that it was not an immutable
law of nature that horse-archers should run out
of arrows, and that if you used archers it would
be a good thing to give them something to shoot
with. It sounds very simple; but if we substitute
shells for arrows, and take our minds back to
1914, we may perhaps think that it was not quite
as simple as it sounds. Surenas took advantage
of the loose feudal system of Parthia and his own
wealth to create a private army of his own to

carry out his ideas. He thought he could muni-
tion 10,000 men[1]; so he raised 10,000 horse-
archers from his retainers, and—this was the
vital matter—he formed a corps of 1000 Arabian
camels, that is, swift camels who could accompany cavalry on the march[2]; these carried the
reserve arrows, one camel to every ten men.
I do not know how many arrows a camel can
carry—some statistician might like to work it
out—but when its trial came the army was able
to shoot as it pleased throughout the afternoon
and evening of a long summer's day. This force
is said to have accompanied Surenas everywhere[3], which means that it was constantly
being trained; it was in fact a small highly
trained professional army, extremely mobile,

[1] Taken literally, Plutarch (*Crassus*, 21) seems to mean
9000 archers and 1000 cataphracts; but there can be no
doubt that the knights were not part of Surenas' private
army and had merely been put under his command for
the campaign against Crassus, and little doubt that
Plutarch's 10,000 really refers to the private army, the
1000 camels implying a round figure. Plutarch has
probably confused the figures in his source.

[2] See Appendix III.

[3] No doubt in peace-time he took his harem about
with him also, and the camels carried other things than
arrows; but he did not take the ladies and their im-
pedimenta to fight Crassus.

depending solely on long-range weapons, and
with a supply of ammunition which was proved
by the event to be adequate for a first-class battle.
Nothing like this had ever been seen in the
world before, and I do not know when anything like it was next seen again. At Carrhae this
force encountered a Roman army more than
three times its size and poured arrows into it
with impunity till nightfall, leaving the sur-
vivors so demoralised that it was easy to gather
them in afterwards. Crassus never had a chance;
and if Caesar had been there, with no more
cavalry than Crassus had, he would not have had
a chance either.

Carrhae is perhaps the most astonishing of all
the battles of this age, because the idea of depending on long-range weapons with unlimited
ammunition is so intensely modern. It ought to
have revolutionised the world's warfare; but in
fact it produced little effect, for Surenas was put
to death next year and his organisation broken
up. All that can be said is that long-range weapons
did acquire a little more importance; the Parthians in their campaign against Antony must
have had *some* sort of a reserve of arrows, and
the Romans took *some* steps to counter the

horse-archer by means of the expert slinger, whose weapon, with lead bullets, could out-range the bow. But for the matter now under consideration, the development of cavalry, Carrhae possesses little importance; it was just an extraordinary flash from one man's brain, which came long before its time.

This concludes the subject of cavalry itself; but something must be added about an arm re-lated to cavalry—elephants. The years between Alexander's death and the battle of Magnesia in 190 B.C. constitute the period, I believe the only period in history, in which the elephant played an important part in the warfare of the West. Many animals beside horses and camels have been used in war, as Lucretius guessed, though his instances were not very happy[1]. Aeneas twice mentions the use of wasps[2]. It was common in Hellenistic times to employ dogs as fortress guards. The Spaniards killed Hamilcar Barca by firing their ox-wagons and sending them against him while they attacked from behind the blazing line[3], a thing which his son Hannibal must have remembered when by means of a herd of oxen

[1] v, 1308 *sqq*: bulls, boars and lions.
[2] XXXVII, 4; LIV.   [3] Appian, *Iber.* 5.

he escaped from Fabius' trap; both feats can be paralleled in the history of South Africa[1]. Of modern aids, the Romans added the carrier pigeon[2], and we ourselves the white mouse. But the elephant was a serious fighting weapon. The West first made its acquaintance in Alexander's battle on the Hydaspes against Porus, for the elephants at Gaugamela were not in action. This was quite unlike Alexander's other battles; as untrained horses will not face elephants he was unable himself to help his army, beyond defeating Porus' cavalry and preventing them from interfering. In most of his battles he saved his men all he could by using his brains; he never, if he could by any means avoid it, fought a battle like Pyrrhus' battles with the Romans, in which the two sides merely hammered each other till something gave way. But against the two hundred elephants of Porus he had no choice; all

[1] In 1510 d'Almeida was killed near Table Bay by Hottentots, who attacked and assegaied the Portuguese from behind a screen of oxen; see G. M. Theal, *The Beginning of South African History*, p. 178. Did the Boer leaders in the South African War recall this incident when they employed herds of oxen to break a way through barbed wire?
[2] Pliny, *N.H.* x, 110.

he could do was to put some of his best infantry
in line and leave it to them. They did defeat the
elephants, but it was evidently a fearful struggle.
The men were never quite the same again, and
from that battle dates the growing weariness
which led to the mutiny on the Beas; while
the impression made on the generals, and particularly upon Seleucus, who had led the line,
was that elephants were an arm to be obtained
at any price, and after Alexander's death every
one of the contending generals got all the elephants he could. When settled kingdoms formed
and Indian elephants became a Seleucid mono-
poly, other States turned their attention to
Africa, and soon after 280 B.C. both Carthage and
the Ptolemies in Egypt were training African
elephants. The Carthaginians got theirs from
North Africa, the Ptolemies from the Red Sea
hinterland north of Abyssinia and from Ethiopia.
Both states imported Indian trainers to teach
the elephants, as has been done in our time by
the Belgians on the Congo; at Carthage the
Indians also guided the elephants in action, but
one would expect to find in Egypt (though there
is no evidence as yet) that the Indians founded a
school of riders from among Ptolemy's subjects,

just as the Tamil trainers on the Congo have
now taught African natives.

There is a modern belief that the elephant was
the tank of antiquity[1]. In fact, the elephant had
three uses in war—to act as a screen against the
enemy cavalry, to attack the enemy infantry, and
to break into a fortified position; this last is the
only function which can be compared with that
of the tank, and it was generally unsuccessful;
any sort of fortification could easily hold up
elephants, the usual plan being to pick off the
drivers and to put down caltrops which lamed
the animals. The Macedonians began by using
elephants to break into fortified places. Perdiccas did this in his campaign against Ptolemy,
and Polyperchon at the siege of Megalopolis,
where, after he had breached the wall with a
tunnel and his infantry had been beaten back
from the breach, he sent forward the elephants
to try and force a passage; but both attempts
were complete failures, and the Macedonian
world never used elephants in that way again.
At a later time the Carthaginians tried to force

[1] Captain and Brevet-Major H. G. Eady, R.E., "The
Tank," *United Services Journal*, 1926, p. 81. I think I have
met this idea elsewhere, but have not the reference.

the Roman trenches outside Panormus with elephants; they failed in the same way. The only successful use of the elephant as a tank known to me is in the war between Carthage and her revolted mercenaries, when the elephants stormed the mercenaries' camp. To compare elephants with tanks is, in my opinion, quite misleading.

The Macedonian Powers used their elephants almost entirely as a screen against cavalry. The classical instance is Ipsus, where the 480 elephants which Seleucus brought into action formed a screen which prevented Demetrius, after his victorious cavalry charge, from returning to the battlefield, though his horses were trained to elephants. Another case probably is the victory which Antiochus I won over the Gauls in Asia Minor in 275. When the Gauls invaded Asia Antiochus ordered his general in Bactria to get him twenty elephants from India; his orders were so urgent that the elephants came on to him from Babylonia a month in advance of the accompanying troops, and he took them straight across the Taurus; four were footsore, but he took the other sixteen into action and defeated the Gauls in the so-called Elephant

Victory. So far as can be made out, the part they played was to prevent the excellent Gallic cavalry from taking any part in the battle, their horses not being trained to elephants. The battle which ought to throw most light on the use of elephants is Paraitakene, which I have quoted so often, for both Antigonus and Eumenes had a strong force of Indian elephants. Unfortunately, so far as concerns the elephants, Diodorus' transcript from Hieronymus seems to be very imperfect, and we can only make out vaguely that both generals meant to use their elephants as screens against the enemy cavalry, and perhaps to threaten that cavalry in turn. A development of the screen idea was shown by Pyrrhus at Heraclea, where he used his elephants to protect the flanks of his phalanx. The use of elephants threw an enormous burden on the cavalry officers, for every horse had to be trained to them if the cavalry was to remain efficient; but it seems always to have been successfully done, as one would expect from the men of that time.

Judging from the battle between Alexander and Porus, the use of elephants in Indian warfare was to attack the enemy infantry; and the reason why Alexander used such a small part of his heavy infantry in this battle must be that he knew (perhaps Taxiles had told him) that it was vital to have the men in open order, with plenty of room. Among the Macedonian generals the use of elephants to attack infantry was a very secondary matter; but it became the regular function of the African elephants of Carthage, though largely by accident. In the battle between the Carthaginians and Regulus, the Spartan Xanthippus, who commanded the Carthaginians, had no need of his elephants as a cavalry screen, since he possessed overwhelming cavalry; he went back therefore to the Indian tactics and sent forward his elephants in advance of the phalanx; Regulus did not know that open order was the way to meet them, and they ploughed through the massed legionaries with tremendous effect. Naturally Carthage followed this up; in her war with the mercenaries the elephants were victorious again and again, and to them Carthage in no small degree owed her salvation. These successes reacted on the Macedonian Powers, and at Raphia in 217 B.C. the elephants were no longer used as cavalry screens; on the left wing they fought with each other, and the victorious Indian elephants of Antiochus passed on to break the Egyptian line. This is the only recorded battle in which Indian and African elephants ever met; the Africans were defeated, but as they were heavily outnumbered no deductions of any kind can be drawn. Polybius' explanation of the defeat, that the African elephants were smaller and weaker than the Indian, is a mere repetition of a silly remark originally made by Ctesias, which continued to be copied by one writer from another for centuries after the African elephant was well known, a lamentable example of what literary men *can* do; and the recorded weights of tusks show that the African elephants of the Ptolemies were at least as good animals as those of to-day[1]. So far as any difference in military efficiency can be detected between the two species it is probably slightly in favour of the African elephants of Carthage. They failed at Zama, because Scipio knew how to meet them; it seems as if elephants soon lost their terrors for experienced troops, but they could be deadly the *first* time, which enhances the achievement of Alexander's men on the Hydaspes.

The last really serious use of elephants was

[1] On this story see Tarn, *Class. Quart.* xx, 1926, p. 98.

at Magnesia in 190; their last recorded employment, I think, was at the battle of Thapsus in the
Roman civil wars. After this the Romans gave
them up, while the Parthians never used them at
all. Their use in battle by Europeans was one of
those remarkable phenomena of the Hellenistic
period which did not survive its close, blazing
up and dying out like new stars; we shall meet
with a parallel in naval warfare in the next
lecture.

Lecture III

SIEGE WARFARE[1] & NAVAL WARFARE

I MUST now deal with the use of machines in war, which means siege warfare and naval warfare. The developments which I sketched in the first two lectures were due to the Macedonian and the Asiatic; but the story of machines—siege trains and ships—is largely one of Greek brains, though often in Macedonian service. This illustrates both the driving power of the Macedonian and the tremendous pressure exerted by war, for, apart from military needs, Greeks invented next to nothing in the way of machinery; the Greek mind, perhaps happily for itself, did not work that way.

It had been very difficult in classical Greece to take a walled city. They had some sort of battering ram—Pericles used one at Samos; scaling ladders were known, and tunnelling

[1] Best now is E. Schramm, *Poliorketik*, in Kromayer and Veith, *op. cit.* See also R. Schneider, *Geschütze* in Pauly-Wissowa. These will give the older literature.

[101]

under the wall; a mound of earth might be raised against the wall, as the Spartans did at Plataea. But speaking generally, you either tried to starve a city out, or relied on your friends inside; a large part of Aeneas' military manual, written about 350 for commanders of besieged cities, is taken up with devices to circumvent the friends of the besiegers inside the wall, and even Philip secured nearly every city he took through treachery. But the later Assyrian kings had known more than this; beside rams, they had used towers to raise their archers to the level of the battlements, and they had regularly taken walled cities in a way which Greeks before Philip's time were quite unable to do. What was known in Assyria was also known, by bitter experience, in Syria and Phoenicia, and so passed to Carthage; and down to 400 B.C. the Carthaginians knew more about sieges than any Greek.

The first Greek to possess a full siege apparatus is said to have been Dionysius of Syracuse, who at the siege of Motye in 398 B.C. had towers, rams, and arrow-firing catapults; his artisans came from many countries, including the sphere of Carthage, and his towers and rams were probably modelled on Carthaginian practice; that is, the knowledge which came to him had travelled along a line Assyria–Phoenicia–Carthage–Sicily, leaving Greece in a backwater, where she remained till Philip of Macedon appeared. Philip first employed a full siege apparatus at the siege of Perinthus in 341 B.C.; it is not known where he got it from, or how the gap between Dionysius and himself is to be bridged, though Xenophon had certainly *heard* of towers[1]. But the real problem is the invention of the torsion catapult.

The catapult developed from the bow, and like all such things must have advanced gradually from the less complicated to the more complicated form. One of the uses of a shield was to stop an arrow; consequently, to pierce a shield you had to increase the force of the arrow, which meant increasing the spring-back of the bow which propelled it. But the amount of spring-back you can obtain from a hand-bow is limited by the strength of a man's arm; hence the next step must be the crossbow. In the mediaeval crossbow mechanical devices were used to stretch the string; in the Greek crossbow, called

---

[1] *Cyrop.* VI, I, 52–5, the movable towers with Cyrus' army.

gastraphetes, invented by Zopyrus of Tarentum, the stretching was done by the man pressing a sliding muzzle against the ground with his body[1]. The *gastraphetes* is never mentioned by historians, and cannot have been much used; for Greeks never knew of the steel bow, on which the mediaeval crossbow depended for its effect. The next step was to mount the crossbow on a stand, make the bow part still stronger, and stretch the string by a windlass or other mechanical means; this was now a catapult, καταπέλτης, which only means something which, unlike the hand-bow, would pierce a πέλτη or shield. This catapult with a bow was superseded by the torsion catapult, in which the power was obtained, not by the resilience of a bent bow, but by the uncoiling of twisted cables; there were two forms, one firing arrows and one firing stones. I will describe the torsion catapult presently.

The arrow-firing catapult is said to have been invented at Syracuse for Dionysius about 400 B.C.; but its progress was so slow that it was probably not the torsion catapult but the less effective catapult with a bow, which naturally came

[1] H. Diels, *Antike Technik,* 2nd ed. 1920, p. 22, has a good description.

first. A catapult arrow was shown at Sparta as a
curiosity about 370 B.C.[1]; an inscription mentions
two catapults at Athens about 358–4 B.C.[2];
Aeneas, writing about 350 B.C., only mentions
catapults once, and couples them with slings[3].
On the other hand, in 341 B.C. both Philip
and Byzantium possessed plenty of arrow-firing
catapults, but no stone-throwers. Our first firm
ground is that the stone-thrower, which was
quite certainly a torsion catapult, first appears
in history at Alexander's siege of Tyre (for the
mention of stone-throwers in the Second Book
of Chronicles[4] can hardly be earlier); and as its

[1] Plutarch, *Mor.* 219 A.

[2] *I.G.* II², 120, l. 37 (358–7 or 354–3 B.C.). A καταπαλταφέτας is known at Athens of about this period, Dittenberger, *Syll.*[3] 1249.

[3] XXXII, 8; doubtless as being the two weapons which would outrange a bow. For the same reason, when Alexander got his catapults out on the ramp at Aornos (see *post*) he sent slingers with them, the only occasion on which he seems to have attached much importance to slingers.

[4] XXVI, 15, "Engines...to shoot arrows and great stones withal." There seems general agreement that Chronicles cannot be earlier than 333 (Alexander), while some put it after 300; see the collection of opinions in Canon Driver's *Introduction to the Literature of the Old Testament.* Mr J. C. Gadd tells me that no allusion to a catapult has been found in Assyrian literature.

invention is not one of those ascribed to his engineer Diades, Alexander must have obtained it through the Phoenician workmen he collected, which bears out Pliny's statement (*N.H.* VII, 201) that the stone-thrower was invented in Phoenicia. But whether the utilisation of the *principle* of torsion—and that is the important matter—was discovered in Phoenicia, or Sicily, or where, cannot be said; all we can say is that it was known before Alexander.

Though Philip's two great sieges failed, while Alexander never had a failure, it is from Philip that scientific siege warfare dates, so far as concerns the Greek world; and during the two generations after him methods and machines were perfected, both for attack and defence. There was a race in development between the siege engine and the wall, and it cannot be said definitely that either won; Alexander took Tyre, but Demetrius failed to take Rhodes, as did Polyperchon to take Megalopolis; Rome took Carthage, but failed to take Syracuse till the defenders made her a present of it. But apparently on balance the defence finally had rather the worst of it. Philip already possessed the three main weapons, towers, rams, catapults; Alexander's Thessalian engineer Diades, the "man who took Tyre with Alexander" as a papyrus calls him[1], improved the towers and rams and added the boarding-bridge; in the hands of Demetrius the Besieger and his Greek engineers Epimachus and Hegetor the tower, the ram, and the stone-throwing catapult reached their highest development. Nothing further on these lines seems to have been possible; Roman siege-work was only a copy of Graeco-Macedonian siege-work, and the one addition of first-rate importance made to Demetrius' technique prior to the discovery of gunpowder was the invention of Greek fire at Constantinople.

The city wall, the object of attack, had altered greatly. Walls had often been built of brick, on a stone foundation, with wooden battlements. But brick was now useless against the modern ram, as was wood against the stone-throwing catapult; a first-class city, and many cities even of the second or third class, had walls of solid stone, with stone battlements, and as thick and high as they could be built. When Philip V came south with a splendidly equipped siege train to take Phthiotic Thebes, which he did easily, he

[1] *Laterculi Alexandrini*, given by Diels, *op. cit.* p. 30.

failed on his way to take quite a little town, Melitaea in Oeta, because its wall was too high for his ladders and he did not wish to waste time battering it down. The wall was divided into sections by square stone towers, a bowshot apart, and along the top from tower to tower ran a pathway protected by stone battlements; in a great fortress this pathway might be covered in with a stone roof, but probably the roof and fittings were often of wood, which were removed when hostilities broke out to avoid the risk of fire, like the wooden fittings of a modern battleship. The towers and battlements would be equipped with large numbers of catapults and stone-throwers. Outside the wall was a deep ditch, to hinder the approach of rams; a great fortress might have three ditches, and at Syracuse the outside ditch, which has been partly traced, was 160 yards from the wall[1], effective shooting range being some 200 yards; the catapults on the wall thus covered the outside ditch.

The assault had to begin by filling in the ditches, to enable the tower and rams to be brought up to the walls; this had to be done under catapult fire from the walls. In the fully

[1] Schramm, *Röm. Mitt.* XL, 1925, p. 3.

developed technique used by Demetrius at Rhodes his sappers worked behind enormous shields called tortoises, each one reached through a covered gallery whose entrance was out of shot; as the ground was levelled the tortoises approached the wall, and when it was reached the sappers tunnelled under it. A chamber was then hollowed out under the wall; this was propped up by wooden supports till the work was finished, when the sappers fired the supports and withdrew. This might bring down part of the wall, as happened in Polyperchon's siege of Megalopolis and Philip V's siege of Abydos; but usually the besieged met the tunnel in time with a counter-tunnel, followed by hand-to-hand fighting underground; in the siege of Rhodes the Rhodians erected barriers in the tunnels, which they succeeded in holding. Of greater importance than tunnelling were the towers and the rams. The ram was a tree-trunk with an iron head and beak, either running on rollers or swung from a support by chains; Alexander at Tyre must have used rams mounted on ships, the only case known. Hegetor's two rams, used by Demetrius at Rhodes, were plated with iron to prevent them buckling; each was

worked by 1000 men through a great shield. The
account we have calls them 120 cubits long; but
it is believed that rams of 180 feet would certainly buckle, and, as I explained before (pp. 15,
16), they were probably short cubits, say some
130 feet, which is still an enormous length.

The actual breaching of the wall depended on
the rams; the use of the great towers, called
Helepoleis, "Takers of cities," was to destroy the
battlements and their artillery and prevent the
defenders from disabling the rams, whether by
dropping stones upon them or by catching the
head in a noose and drawing it up. The tower
had therefore to be at least as high as the wall.
The highest ever built are supposed to be the
two which Alexander used on his mole at Tyre,
for the top of the wall at Tyre was 150 feet above
sea-level, but they did not contribute much to
the capture of the city; probably the one con-
structed by Epimachos and used by Demetrius
at Rhodes was more efficient. It was about
60 feet high, built in diminishing stages, with
two ladders between each stage for ascent and
descent; the lower stages carried heavy stone
throwers, the higher light catapults; on each
stage was a water-tank in case of fire. It ran on

pivoted wheels which would turn in any direction, and needed several thousand men to move it. The old protection against fire, raw hides, which was still used on Alexander's towers, had been replaced by an armouring of iron plates; the artillery fired through portholes, which could be closed by bags of hide stuffed with wool to protect the gunners against stones. But when it went into action the Rhodian stone-throwers knocked off some of the armour plates, and it was then set on fire by flame-carriers and withdrawn. Another way of dealing with towers was to mine under them and thus throw them down.

Towers had another use besides carrying artillery; they sometimes carried a boarding-bridge, which could be let down on to the wall to enable the troops in the tower to get a footing on it; an instance is Alexander's tower at Massaga, where however the bridge broke. But the real use of the boarding-bridge was in attacking a wall from the sea. It was apparently invented by Alexander's engineer Diades, as appears by combining three things: Athenaeus says Diades invented the κόραξ[1]; Polybius (I, 22) says a

---

[1] περὶ μηχανημάτων (ed. Schneider, *Gött. Abh.* 1912), 10, ll. 10 *sqq.*

boarding-bridge was called κόραξ; and the first boarding-bridges known are those used by Alexander at Tyre. Alexander's bridges were carried on two merchant ships, which would stand the weight, and were lowered on to the wall where part of it had been breached, thus enabling picked troops to assault. Similar bridges, called *sambucae*, each carried on two quinqueremes lashed together and hoisted by tackle and pulleys attached to the masts, were used by Marcellus at the siege of Syracuse; but they had no success, for Archimedes either tore them loose from the ships with grapnels, or smashed them by dropping great stones, which were slung out over the battlements by means of long poles with a compensating weight at the other end.

But the high-water mark of ancient mechanics was certainly the torsion catapult[1]. It was perfected before 300 B.C. and constituted the artillery of the world till the invention of gunpowder; it held its own against cannon for a considerable time, and as late as 1727 a French military writer[2] advocated its revival on the ground that

[1] My description is taken from Schramm.
[2] The Chevalier de Folard, in his commentary to Dom Thuillier's *Polybius* (cited by Sir R. Payne-Gallwey, *The*

it was more accurate than the cannon of his day, as well as cheaper. There were two types: the catapult proper, καταπέλτης, of various sizes, shooting different sized arrows, and the stone-thrower, πετροβόλος or λιθοβόλος, also of various sizes; but the principle of both was the same. The torsion catapult had a long wooden stock, with a groove to carry the arrow or stone; across the front end, replacing the bow, was a vertical wooden shield with the torsion cables at either extremity, mounted vertically in the frame-work, rather like great cylinders. Each set was composed of two very thick skeins of material with a great number of threads in each skein, which gave more power than solid cables; the two skeins were twisted tight round each other by mechanical means, and also strained to the utmost between the top and bottom of the frame. Into each pair was inserted the end of a wooden arm, replacing the two ends of the bow; these arms carried the bowstring. When the bowstring was drawn down by windlasses in loading, the arms followed, twisting the

Crossbow, p. 273). De Folard however was somewhat crazy about catapults; see Ch. Liskenne and J. B. B. Sauvan, *Bibliothèque historique et militaire*, III, p. 796.

already twisted skeins yet further; the release of the bowstring permitted them to uncoil, throwing the arms back with great power. In the heavy stone-throwers, when unloaded, the arms pointed forward, so as to be drawn back through the greatest possible arc. The windlasses for loading were worked by hand by the gunners, and the whole machine, mounted on a stand, had a queer resemblance to a machine-gun and its shield.

The straining of the skeins necessitated the use of a material which would stand stretching, and the two favourite materials were women's hair and sinews of animals, except pigs[1]; horsehair was only a substitute, and Ctesibius' attempt to use metal springs was a failure. In the third century B.C. the trade in women's hair must have been enormous; in 250 Rhodes sent to Sinope for her war with Mithridates about three-quarters of a ton of it[2]; in 225 Seleucus made Rhodes a present of hair weighing at least several tons[3]. Women of the poorer classes everywhere must have sold their hair regularly;

[1] Heron, *Belopoiika*, ed. Diels and Schramm, *Berlin. Abh.* 1918, p. 110, c. 29, and p. 112, c. 30.
[2] Polybius, IV, 56, 3; 300 talents of prepared hair and 100 talents of prepared sinews.
[3] *Ib.* V, 89, 9.

the short-haired girl is not a modern invention. When we read, as in the last siege of Carthage, of women giving their hair for the catapults as though it were something exceptionally patriotic, it means giving it for nothing, and refers especially to wealthy women who did not usually cut their hair.

Information in the technical writers, and experiments, have shown what the range of a catapult was [1]. As late as Wellington's time there was practically no chance of hitting a single man at 100 yards with a musket, if you aimed at him. But the best arrow-firing catapults could be trusted to kill a single man at 100 yards, and to hit a group of men at 200 yards; if well elevated they might carry for 500 yards, but had no accuracy and little power. The big stone-throwers would carry effectively for 200 yards, the effect of the stone being due to weight, not to muzzle velocity; I do not know with what accuracy, but they were accurate at short ranges. The heaviest stone thrown was a talent—between 50 and 60 pounds; it was no good against a first-class wall, but it was effective against other machines or groups of men, and would breach

[1] The ranges here given are from Schramm.

any improvised wall, as was done in Demetrius'
fight for the mole at Rhodes. Archimedes con-
structed a stone-thrower to throw a stone of
three talents; doubtless it worked, but nothing
so large is actually recorded in use. The defence
against the stone-thrower was to hang out bags
of any soft stuff; sometimes too a number of
iron chains were hung out, a device used in the
American Civil War by the Federal cruiser
Kearsage in her fight with the *Alabama*.

Very important was the flame-carrier, used
for setting on fire the wood-work of the enemy
machines; its basis was oil or naphtha in some
form enclosed in a cylinder, and it was apparently
fired from the stone-throwing catapult. I have
not met with any exact description of how it
worked, but it was a much-trusted weapon and
was evidently effective; during the last night
of Demetrius' grand attack upon Rhodes the
Rhodians fired off 800 flame-carriers, the cylinders being subsequently collected and counted,
and they managed to set fire to Demetrius'
armoured tower at a point where some plating
had been knocked off, which shows that the stone-
throwers were pretty accurate at short range.

Beside the catapult there was another torsion

stone-thrower, called μονάγκων or One-arm, less elaborate, which worked without a string and with a single horizontal pair of torsion cables; the stone was held by an arm, and the arm, which was fixed in the cables, was wound down to a horizontal position and then released; it flung the stone like a man's arm, and was then checked by a crossbar. This form is never actually described till Roman times, though it was certainly Hellenistic; but it is well known from mediaeval pictures and seems to be the popular idea of a catapult[1]. It would throw a considerable distance, but had no pretensions to accuracy, and probably played little part in Hellenistic warfare.

Though no improvements, except in details, were ever made upon the catapults of Demetrius' time, the science of Alexandria did make an attempt to discover new principles. Dionysius of Alexandria made a repeating catapult, called *polybolon*, in which the firing of the string loaded a new arrow; but it would only carry a short distance. Ctesibius, beside his attempt to use

---

[1] The experiments made in this country by Sir R. Payne-Gallwey were with One-arms; see his book *The Crossbow*, 1903.

metal springs to replace the torsion cables, also tried to use compressed air, like a modern air-gun. His air-catapult[1] had an old-fashioned bow, and to each end of the bow was attached a cylinder in which worked a close-fitting piston; when the ends of the bow were drawn down in loading they pushed down the pistons, and when the catapult was fired the compressed air drove up the pistons and with them the ends of the bow. But it could not compete with the torsion catapult, and neither it nor the repeating catapult came into practical use.

The sieges of this period and the enormous bulk of material of every kind employed by both sides suggest that a quite disproportionate amount of the energy of every city must have been wasted in constructing machines of war and heaping up ammunition. Rhodes was a city of peaceable merchants, but even Demetrius, whose ideas were not small, was astounded at the amount of artillery they brought into action; Carthage in 149 is said to have handed over 2000 catapults and stone-throwers, with a vast mass of ammunition for them[2]. We never hear any-

[1] See the description in Diels, *Antike Technik*, p. 106.
[2] Appian, *Lib.* 80.

where of any difficulty incurred in arming men; and even a little city like Abydos could stand a desperate siege. This elaborate siege warfare was a terrible drain upon civilisation on its material side.

Though the catapult was essentially siege artillery, an interesting attempt was made by Alexander to use it as field artillery. He carried arrow-firing catapults with him all over Asia; he never used them in a pitched battle, but the importance he attached to them in irregular warfare, and their effectiveness, were shown on the Jaxartes, where he used them to clear the farther bank, and at Aornos, where he got them up the hill and built his extraordinary ramp across the Burimar ravine in order to bring them into action against the actual stronghold; Sir Aurel Stein has told that story in his book *On Alexander's Track to the Indus*[1]. One can see that Alexander's imagination would be attracted by the idea of field artillery, but only one case is recorded of its use later: in 207 B.C., at the battle of Mantinea between the Achaean League and

[1] My account of this ramp in *Cambridge Ancient History*, VI, written before Stein's brilliant discovery, must now be taken as superseded.

Machanidas of Sparta, Machanidas had catapults in the field, but seemingly they had no influence on the result. The reason usually given why catapults had no future as field artillery is that the strings and torsion cables needed perpetual replacement; also they fired slowly, and took a long time to put together. For when a general carried a siege train with him, as Alexander did across Asia, he usually only took the essential parts of the machines, and all the heavy wooden framework was made afresh when needed[1]; Alexander did not carry completely mounted catapults up the well-wooded Aornos. Philon mentions a small catapult which could be mounted and made ready in an hour[2], but evidently this was regarded as very extraordinary.

And there is no recorded case in the Hellenistic world of catapults being used in a naval battle; that first came in with the Roman civil wars. Both Alexander and Demetrius mounted catapults on warships for the purpose of attacking fortresses, because speed then did not matter;

[1] Antony took an 80-foot ram with him across Armenia to Atropatene, but he was intending to operate in a country short of timber.
[2] Schramm in Kromayer and Veith, *op. cit.* p. 217.

but though the heavy stone-thrower might perhaps have been useful in a naval action, evidently its utility was held insufficient to compensate the great loss of speed involved in carrying it and its ammunition. For warships were very light and crank affairs, and to mount a catapult in the bows depressed the bows, so that the stern had to be ballasted down to correspond, submerging the vessel above its most efficient waterline—efficient, that is, for purposes of rowing; Scipio before Tunes in 203 B.C. decided that it was hopeless to attempt to take his quinqueremes into action, as they had siege engines on board[1]. It was possible, for siege purposes, to mount even a greater weight than catapults on quinqueremes, provided they were lashed together in pairs for stability; Marcellus' boarding-bridges at Syracuse were carried in this way, though it was a failure. But Alexander and Demetrius, if there was any real weight to be carried, always used heavy merchant ships, sometimes also lashed together in pairs. Ships however did many things in sieges which they did not do in battle. Fireships for instance were used; and Demetrius when attacking the har-

[1] Polybius, xiv, 10, 9, a very conclusive passage.

bour at Rhodes protected his ships with a float-
ing armoured boom.

This brings me to naval warfare[1]. Down to
the final destruction of Athenian sea power at
the battle of Amorgos in 322 the standard warship in the Mediterranean had been the trireme;
from Amorgos down to Actium in 31 B.C. the
standard warship was the quinquereme. But the
matter did not end with quinqueremes; for the
late fourth century and the first half of the third
century saw a regular race between the Hellenistic Powers in building larger and larger warships. In the second century the great ships began gradually to fall out of use, not because they
were inefficient, but partly because they were
expensive and needed such large crews, and
partly because the new masters of the Aegean,
Rome and Rhodes, did not use ships larger than
quinqueremes; Antony partially revived them
for a time, but Actium was the end, and the
Roman Empire, with no enemy to fight in the
Mediterranean except pirates, went back to the
trireme as the standard vessel, though a certain
proportion of quinqueremes was still used. The

---

[1] There is no competent work on Hellenistic naval
matters.

great warships were even more entirely a purely
Hellenistic phenomenon than was the use of
elephants in land warfare. The complete story
would probably be impressive, if only as illustra-
ting what men could do with very simple means.

It is unfortunate that most of the story
has perished. We possess no description of a
Hellenistic naval battle between Salamis in 306
and Chios in 201; that is to say, we know nothing at all of the battles between Egypt and
Macedonia, in which much larger ships took
part than any that fought in the battles of which
we possess accounts. If an even tolerable
account had survived of, let us say, the battle of
Cos, about 258, in which Macedonia deprived
Egypt of the command of the sea, everything
that has been written about ancient naval warfare would have had to be written from a somewhat different angle; we have to try and imagine
it for ourselves as best we can. These great ships
were designated in Greek by words compounded
of a number followed by the termination -ηρης;
there are no words in English, just as there were
none in Latin, to translate these terms, and it is
simplest just to call the ships by their numbers
—a ten, a fifteen, and so on. The numbers are

power-ratios; a *pentekaidekeres* or fifteen was a
ship whose motive power, in relation to that of a
quinquereme, was considered to be expressed by
the proportion 15 to 5. I will consider presently
what it means; but first I must take the quinquereme.

And here I would like to make one suggestion. When we think of a ship, we are apt to
think of something very solid—a liner, a battleship, and so on. A Greek naval fighting machine
was anything but solid; and I would ask you for
a few minutes to forget all you know about ships
and to think of a glorified racing eight. That is
an exaggeration, of course, but it is one which I
have found useful myself as a better line of approach to the matter than the modern associa-
tions of the word "ship."

There is plenty of evidence that a quinquereme
was a comparatively light machine of shallow
draught and low freeboard, and rather crank[1];
it was heavier and stronger than a trireme, but
could be drawn ashore anywhere by hand,
though not so easily as a trireme. If you had

[1] Collected by me in "The Greek Warship," *J.H.S.*
xxv, 1905, pp. 137, 204, to which I refer here once for all.
Except for some remarks about the great ships, of which
I then knew little, the essentials of this paper are valid.

looked down on a quinquereme from the air,
the stern and bow erections being supposed
to be removed, you would have seen a sort of
oblong frame, long and narrow, with quite
straight sides; the curving sides of the hull below would be invisible, but emerging from the
frame, like the head and tail of a tortoise, would
be a pointed bow at one end and a more or less
pointed stern at the other. It was impossible to
equalise the leverage of the oars if rowed along the
curving side of the ship; and the straight sides
of the oblong I have described, through which
the oars were rowed, acted as a sort of con-
tinuous outrigger and equalised the leverage. The
Greek term for this outrigger is παρεξειρεσία;
the meaning of the word was Assmann's discovery[1], and is the most illuminating thing discovered in modern times about these warships;
it is certainly correct, and I may mention that
excellent diagrams exist of the Maltese quinqueremes used by the Knights of St John which
show the same arrangement[2]. The quinquereme
was rowed by a single row of oars through oar-

[1] *Seewesen* in Baumeister's *Denkmäler*. Of course triremes had a similar outrigger.
[2] Furtenbach, *Architectura Navalis*, 1629.

holes in the outrigger, with five men to each oar;
and the rowers were divided horizontally into
three working squads, as was done both in triremes and in the greatest Hellenistic ships—
thranites in the stern, zugites amidships, thalamites in the bows[1]. There was a deck over the
rowers' heads, and the sides of the outrigger
were carried up to this deck to protect the
rowers from arrows. All ships larger than triremes, and some triremes, now had their rowers
protected in the same way; a vessel so built was
called a cataphract, which means covered in. It
follows that no painted or sculptured representation of a Hellenistic warship ever will be or can
be found which shows the arrangement of the
rowers[2], because they were completely invisible.
As to the oars, I have mentioned that a quin-

[1] See Appendix IV, which supplements what I wrote in
"The Greek Warship" and in *Class. Rev.* xx, 1906, p. 75.
It must be remembered that this or that Byzantine com-
mentator may have misunderstood κάτω and ἄνω, which
mean fore and aft (*J.H.S.* 1905, p. 145), and thought of
thranites up top, etc., exactly like many modern writers;
but this has no bearing on the realities of the matter.

[2] Naturally the pleasure barge from Lake Nemi has
no bearing on this. There are several photographs of this
hulk in the *Illustrated London News* for July–December,
1929, pp. 155, 818.

quereme was rowed by five men to the oar, like the quinqueremes of Malta and Venice; the outrigger alone would make this certain, though Assmann never saw the necessary implications of his own discovery. I collected much of the evidence in my old paper on *The Greek Warship* already mentioned; but I may give one passage which is conclusive, because everybody has overlooked it, including myself. Polybius, in his account of the siege of Syracuse, has occasion to mention the oarage—ταρσός or εἰρεσία (he uses both terms)—of one side of a quinquereme. Livy, who is good on ships, translated the passage and rendered εἰρεσία, not by *ordines remorum*, as he must have done had there been several rows of oars, but by *ordo remorum*[1]; there

---

[1] Polybius, VIII, 4 (6), 2, ὀκτὼ πεντήρεσι, παραλελυμέναις τοὺς ταρσούς, ταῖς μὲν τοὺς δεξιούς, ταῖς δὲ τοὺς εὐωνύμους, καὶ συνεζευγμέναις πρὸς ἀλλήλας σύνδυο κατὰ τοὺς ἐψιλωμένους τοίχους, προσῆγον πρὸς τὸ τεῖχος διὰ τῆς τῶν ἐκτὸς τοίχων εἰρεσίας κ.τ.λ., cf. 4 (6), 7, διὰ τῆς εἰρεσίας τῆς ἀφ᾽ ἑκατέρου τῶν ἐκτὸς ταρσῶν. Livy, XXIV, 34, 6, "Junctae aliae binae quinqueremes demptis interioribus remis, ut latus lateri adplicaretur, cum exteriore ordine remorum velut una navis agerentur," etc. *Ordo remorum* seems to be the translation of εἰρεσία rather than of ταρσός; but it is immaterial which, as both words are general terms for "oarage" and Polybius here uses them without distinction for the oarage of one side of a quinquereme.

was only one row of oars. Even the latest
German writer, A. Koester, has practically
abandoned the old theory of superposed banks
for anything larger than triremes[1]. That theory
—a misunderstanding of certain texts conse-
crated by endless repetition—was a mechanical
impossibility, for triremes no less than for quinqueremes; it involved the belief that Zeus, or
some appropriate deity, performed a miracle
every time a warship put to sea. I only mention
it because a new Ptolemaic papyrus has supplied
some valuable evidence[2]. Put very briefly, this
papyrus shows that the term *dikrotos* meant a
triakontor—a small warship with 15 one-man
oars on each side—or a vessel of about that size.
Now we are expressly told that a *dikrotos* had
two divisions of rowers of the same *nature* as the
three divisions in a trireme; and the only possible
division of the rowers in a triakontor was into
fore and aft squads; the trireme therefore follows
suit—precisely as I said must be the case, twenty-
five years ago.

[1] *Das antike Seewesen*, 1923, p. 144; "Das Seekriegs-
wesen bei den Griechen," in Kromayer and Veith, *op. cit.*,
p. 183. Koester, like every text-book writer, makes no
attempt to treat the Hellenistic period.
[2] See Appendix IV.

The quinquereme, as one would expect from
its build, was not really a seaworthy ship in our
sense. If handled with sufficient skill, and kept
head to wind, it might ride out a good deal of
sea, and sometimes did; but often enough no
skill could save it; Demetrius lost most of his
fleet in 295, and a whole Seleucid fleet once went
to the bottom, though it was drawn entirely
from the competent seamen of the Greek cities
of Asia Minor. In incompetent hands, like the
Roman pilots of the first Punic war, a storm
meant almost certain death. But at least we may
honour the courage of the men who put to sea
and fought in such machines.

The invention of the quinquereme was the
great step from which everything else followed,
for it meant the substitution of one big oar
rowed by several men for the three small
grouped oars of a trireme, with their tholes all
on the same level and each rowed by one man[1].

---

[1] As I understand the evidence, the "trireme question" has long been settled, and the only point open to-
day is whether the Greek trireme resembled Admiral
Fincati's very efficient trireme (*i.e.* the Venetian system),
in which the three rowers sat on the same level, or the
trireme of Dr A. B. Cook and the late Mr Wigham
Richardson (*Class. Rev.* XIX, 1905, p. 371), in which the

Livy reflects the change in calling triremes *minoris formae* and the ships with great oars *majoris formae*[1], for to a spectator the difference in appearance would be very marked. There is the same difficulty over the invention of the quinquereme as over that of the catapult: Dionysius of Syracuse is said to have had quadriremes and quinqueremes, and they are not heard of again for two generations. The first fixed point is that in 332 Alexander found quinqueremes in regular use by the Cyprians and Phoenicians; these were certainly true quinqueremes, for not much later—probably in 314— the Phoenicians went on to build *heptereis*,

rower nearest the centre line of the ship sat a *little* higher than No. 2 and No. 2 a *little* higher than No. 1; Mr Wigham Richardson (whose firm built the *Mauretania*) told me that it had been tried out and went very well. Both reconstructions of course put the three tholes on the same level, the vital point. I prefer Fincati's myself, because (*a*) the rowers need less space, (*b*) it proved itself at Venice, (*c*) the tradition may never have quite perished (cf. the catapult), *and* (*d*) Dr Cook échelonned his seats because he thought the thranites, etc., were *rows* and the thranite *had* to be higher than the zugite, etc., which I think is now proved to be wrong.

[1] Livy, XXXVII, 23, 5, *majoris formae* includes sixes and sevens but *not* triremes; XXXVI, 43, 8, *minoris formae* includes *apertae*, *i.e.* triremes and smaller vessels.

sevens, for Demetrius. But Athens in Alexander's time had not yet got the true quinquereme; she was experimenting. She had some quadriremes, built like enlarged triremes with four grouped oars each rowed by one man (it is said that similar quadriremes were used at Venice), and she built seven quinqueremes on the same lines, *i.e.* with five grouped oars; the evidence is the Athenian dockyard inscriptions, which show that at Athens *at this time* the oars of a trireme could be used in a quadrireme and those of a quadrireme in a quinquereme[1]. These quinqueremes were a failure; Athens did not mobilise them for the Lamian War or send them to Salamis. Now if Syracuse had true quinqueremes soon after 400 B.C. all this is incredible; for Corinth usually knew what Syracuse was doing, Athens in the early fourth century was in close touch with Corinth, and, except for Persia, Athens down to 322 was the greatest of naval powers; she could not have neglected the new

---

[1] *I.G.* II², 1632 (II, 812), a, ll. 30–5, c, ll. 233–6, 336 to end (323–322 B.C.). I know of nothing to show whether the ordinary Hellenistic quadrireme continued to have four grouped oars or whether it resembled a quinquereme and had oars each rowed by four men.

discovery for 60 years and then begun retro-grade experiments. The natural conclusion is that the true quinquereme was invented in Cyprus or Phoenicia shortly before Alexander's time, and that if Dionysius ever did possess quinqueremes they were merely experimental things like those of Athens. The probability that the new method of rowing originated in Cyprus or Phoenicia is increased by the fact that so much of the subsequent development of great ships took place in those countries. Pliny, in a list of inventions, part of which is demonstrably wrong, says the quinquereme was invented at Salamis (*N.H.* VII, 208); it may be that a genuine tradition lies behind this, and that the Salamis meant was really Salamis in Cyprus.

The invention of larger ships than quinque-remes was not long delayed. The rapid advance which took place was largely due to Demetrius, though, just as with his siege machines, we do not really know how much was due to him and how much to his naval architects; probably he made suggestions which they translated into fact. The first step was the *heptereis* or sevens, probably invented in 314, which he used with such startling success at the battle of Salamis; by

301 he had a thirteen[1], and thirteen became the largest *class* used[2]; all ships above thirteen— seven are known, not of course including Hieron's ship, which was a glorified merchant- man—were individuals. Demetrius in 288 had a fifteen and a sixteen, famous for their beauty, speed, and efficiency[3]; when he fell, Ptolemy got the fifteen and probably dedicated it at Delos[4], and Lysimachus got the sixteen; it was the flag- ship of his fleet when he died, and was preserved in Macedonia so long as the Antigonid dynasty lasted[5]. Antigonus Gonatas built an even greater

[1] Plutarch, *Dem.* 31, 32.
[2] Callixenus ap. Athen. v, 203 d.
[3] Plutarch, *Dem.* 43. The phrase, *ib.* 20, τὰς μὲν ἑκκαιδεκήρεις αὐτοῦ καὶ τὰς πεντεδεκήρεις ἐθαύμαζον κ.τ.λ. is only an idiom (see Plutarch, *Alex.* 55, l. 4), common enough also in English; there was only one of each.
[4] Tarn, *B.C.H.* XLVI, 1922, p. 473. See P. L. Couchoud's note, *ib.* p. 476.
[5] On Demetrius' fall, Ptolemy and Lysimachus in a sense divided the Aegean; if Ptolemy got Delos and the Cyclades, Lysimachus, with the northern islands, got Samothrace, where seamen brought their offerings to the gods who could save them from the tempest. Ptolemy got the fifteen, but *not* the sixteen; there was no sixteen in the Egyptian navy (Callixenus ap. Athen. v, 203 d). But the sixteen turns up again in Macedonia in 197, when the Romans allowed Philip to keep it (Polybius, XVIII, 44 (27), 6; Livy, XXXIII, 30, 5) as a memorial of an

ship at Corinth, the *Isthmia*[1], described as a three-decker, which led his fleet at Cos; then came the twenty and the thirty of Ptolemy II, built in Cyprus by Pyrgoteles[2], and lastly the forty of Ptolemy Philopator[3].

Now what do these numbers mean? Nobody knows; so I am going to offer an explanation of my own, which does at least correlate all the evidence, and which seems to follow automatically, once the elements of the problem are arranged in proper historical sequence. The material points are these. Demetrius had nothing larger than sevens at Salamis in 306 B.C., while early in 301 he had a thirteen; in between he built an eleven[4], but as he cannot have worked through all the gradations between seven and

older day, like the *Victory*; after Perseus' defeat Aemilius Paulus took it to Rome and made his state entry in it up the Tiber (Livy, XLV, 35). It must then have passed from Demetrius to Lysimachus, and must therefore be the ship which in Memnon, 13, appears as Keraunos' (*i.e.* Lysimachus') flagship. Memnon calls this ship an eight, which misled me for many years; see *post*.

[1] For all details see Tarn, "The Dedicated Ship of Antigonos Gonatas," *J.H.S.* xxx, 1910, p. 209.

[2] Dittenberger, *O.G.I.S.* 39.

[3] Callixenus ap. Athen. v, 203 e *sqq*.

[4] Theophrastus, *Hist. Plant.* v, 8, 1.

thirteen in four years—years of strenuous warfare—we have to account for the possibility that
the eleven and the thirteen were directly derived
from ships not larger than sevens. Next, Lysimachus inspected Demetrius' sixteen[1], and his
big ship, if it was not, as I think, Demetrius'
sixteen itself, was an answer to it; but it is *called*
an eight, which is impossible. This ship helped
to defeat Gonatas[2], and Gonatas' *Isthmia*, which
came later, was in a sense the answer to it;
Pausanias' reference to a nine-fold arrangement
of rowers led me formerly to call it a nine, which
is impossible, for we know that it was more
notable than the fifteen[3] and must therefore represent an advance upon it. The answer to the
Isthmia was Ptolemy's twenty; then came his
thirty, and then Philopator's forty; this suc-
cession of multiples of ten must mean *something*.
There are two other factors. One is that in
the Middle Ages it is said to have been found
impossible to row more than ten men to
an oar; the other is that the one surviving
representation of a great Hellenistic cataphract,

[1] Plutarch, *Dem.* 20.
[2] Memnon, 13.
[3] Pollux, 1, 82; see Tarn, *J.H.S.* xxx, 1910, p. 210.

the Palazzo Spada relief[1], suggests a system of oars grouped in pairs, with the oar-holes échelonned in pairs at slightly different levels, but with the blades making one line in the water.

The explanation then is this. From five to ten the figures mean a single row of oars with so many men to an oar[2]. From eleven to twenty they refer to a system based on oars grouped in pairs, a gigantic bireme; thirteen, for example, meant a system with oars grouped in pairs, each pair being rowed by seven and six men respectively. Lysimachus' ship was not an eight, in the sense of a single row of oars each rowed

[1] Schreiber, *Die hellenistischen Reliefbilder*, x[a], which gives it clearly. This is better than the Villa Ludovisi version, *ib.* xxiii[a].

[2] The galley on the reverses of the numerous series of coins which Antony struck to pay his legions (H. A. Grueber, *Coins of the Roman Republic in the British Museum*, 1910, ii, p. 526) shows quite clearly one single row of oars with the oar-holes in one straight line. The galley thus figured could only be Antony's flagship, which was presumably a ten (Dio Cassius, l, 23, 2; Plutarch, *Ant.* 61); anyhow, it was much larger than a quinquereme (Plutarch, *Ant.* 66). I give this for completeness; the figure ten in the text does not depend upon it, but upon the multiples of ten noticed above.

by eight men, but had a system of oars grouped in pairs, *each* oar with eight men, that is, it was a sixteen, as it ought to have been; I have no doubt that it was really Demetrius' sixteen, for otherwise we cannot account for its preservation in Macedonia. Similarly Gonatas' ship was not a nine, but had a system of oars grouped in pairs, *each* oar with nine men, and was therefore really an eighteen, as it ought to have been[1]; Ptolemy's answer, the twenty, had oars grouped in pairs, each oar with ten men. One could go no further with oars grouped in pairs; so Pyrgoteles, in the thirty, employed a system of oars grouped in *threes*, each oar with ten men; that is, the development of the trireme repeated itself on a monstrous scale. The forty, which was very long, must therefore have attempted a system of oars grouped in *fours*, like the original Athenian quadriremes; and here the thing broke down. By the end of the third century B.C. great ships with grouped oars had ceased to be built and are

---

[1] Professor Adcock suggested to me years ago that this ship might have had more oars (than a nine); he was quite right, but I could not get away from the wrong idea with which I misled myself in 1905 and 1910, that this ship and Lysimachus' ship were abnormal in some way in their oarage. They were not.

[137]

not heard of again[1]; the biggest ship at Chios in 201 was a ten, as it was at Actium. How exactly the oars grouped in pairs were arranged could be ascertained by experiment, but I do not think anyone will ever spend the necessary time or money over it.

I suppose I need hardly say that, except probably the forty, the great ships were thoroughly efficient; I only mention it because so many books, written in the days when Hellenistic history was neglected, have stated the contrary. Both Lysimachus' ship and Antigonus Gonatas' ship *Isthmia* led fleets to victory in battle; in the case of Lysimachus' ship it is recorded that she played the principal part in the success gained[2], and the same is implied for Gonatas' ship. Even for the thirty the matter was settled by the inscription which records the honour paid by Ptolemy II to Pyrgoteles for building her[3], for

---

[1] The Praenestine ship (Koester, *Seewesen*, p. 150) may show that in the Roman Imperial period oars grouped in pairs were sometimes used in small vessels (she cannot of course be larger than a quinquereme, and may be a bireme); but this has nothing to do with the Hellenistic great ships.

[2] Memnon, 13.

[3] Dittenberger, *O.G.I.S.* 39.

that ambitious and hard-headed king, the deviser of the Ptolemaic economic system, would not have honoured a man who designed him something useless; and in fact tradition says another thirty was built[1].

It is possible that we now know the outside dimensions of one of the great ships, probably Demetrius' fifteen. The French excavations at Delos have unearthed a building, decorated with bulls' heads, containing a dock which once housed some dedicated ship much larger than a trireme; the architecture points to Ptolemy I, and probably it housed Demetrius' fifteen when Ptolemy dedicated it[2]. Later on it may or may not have housed the *Isthmia*, which Gonatas dedicated himself. Assuming that it housed Demetrius' fifteen, then the outside dimensions of that vessel, neglecting fractions, were some 162 feet by 29 feet, as against some 120 by 20 for a trireme, the figure given by the docks at Munychia—the Zea docks are longer[3], but the Munychia docks must have sufficed to take a trireme.

[1] Callixenus ap. Athen. v, 203 d.
[2] P. L. Couchoud and J. Svoronos, "Le monument dit 'des Taureaux' à Delos," *B.C.H.* XLV, 1921, p. 270; Tarn, *ib.* XLVI, p. 473.
[3] Possibly they also housed the quadriremes.

The big ship then was substantially longer, as one would expect, and broader in proportion; its length is only $5\frac{1}{2}$ times its breadth, as against 6 times in a trireme. A trireme possibly had more than 25 oar-groups on each side, but it is not known how many of the oars given in the Athenian dockyard lists were spare oars; according to Polybius (1, 26, 7) a quinquereme would have had 30 oars a side, but doubtless some of his 300 "rowers" were really officers and sailors[1]. Perhaps the length of the fifteen as compared to that of a trireme would have admitted 25 of its oar-groups on each side. Certainly as a general thing we cannot suppose much more than 25 oar-groups; not merely because all these galleys were ultimately derived from the pentekontor, but also because the possible length of every galley was strictly limited. Koester has pointed out that the length of a trireme was conditioned by the fact that, if too long, she would break her back between two waves[2]; and there is a good piece of evidence for his view, though he did not quote it. When

---

[1] The Venetian quinqueremes are said to have had 25, 26 or 27 oars a side, but not more.
[2] *Seewesen*, p. 96.

the sea is rough, we think of the waves and say it is running high; a Greek thought of the trough between the waves, and said the sea was hollow; his ancestors had lived in fear of their galleys breaking their backs, just as one of our early destroyers, the *Cobra*, is supposed to have done. The great warships were stronger than a trireme and so could be longer; but similar conditions put a limit to the length; Memnon's account of Lysimachus' ship has doubled the real figures[1], for 50 oar-groups a side would be impossible, both on practical grounds and because the length of her sister ship, the fifteen, is probably known. According to the account we have, Philopator's huge forty would have had 50 oar-groups on each side; here it might possibly be correct, for she had a double hull, something like the old *Calais-Douvres*, and was no more a success than the *Calais-Douvres* was[2].

---

[1] Memnon, 13; 25 oar-groups a side with 8 men at each oar would be $50 \times 16 = 800$ rowers; Memnon has misunderstood Nymphis in some way and turned it into 800 on each side. He is really quite good evidence for 25 oar-groups a side.

[2] She was δίπρωρος and δίπρυμνος; that is, she was an imitation of the common practice of lashing two ships together for stability. Whether the two hulls were built

The naval warfare of the Hellenistic period is not marked by any such complete break with the past as was brought about on land by the emergence of cavalry as the most important arm; the use of a fleet remained what it had been, and the old limitations of the galley were never overcome—its helplessness in the dark, its inability to maintain a blockade or prevent troops crossing the sea. No Power maintained a standing fleet, that is, one always in commission, with one possible exception: Egypt, during the period she was mistress of the Aegean, may have kept a permanent squadron of small cruisers in the archipelago as a police force. What is called the command of the sea, at this time, only meant that the Power who claimed it had a good prospect, if challenged, of getting a fleet to sea which might defeat the challenger. With the rise of the Hellenistic States the strategical centre of naval

together, or only joined afterwards like those of the *Calais-Douvres* (to which I called attention in 1905), cannot be said. Callixenus calls her εὔρυθμος καθ᾽ ὑπερβολήν; but Plutarch (*Dem.* 43) says that in fact she was a failure. A picture of the *Calais-Douvres* was reproduced in *The Times* of 30 Dec. 1929, following a correspondence; the evidence is that she did not roll much, but pitched badly, and could not go out at all in really rough weather.

warfare shifted from the Dardanelles to the south-west corner of Asia Minor, where, speaking very roughly, the spheres of the three great Empires sometimes met; it was in those waters that the command of the Eastern Mediterranean successively passed from Athens to the Macedonian generals, from Egypt to Macedonia, from Antiochus III to Rome and Rhodes; the great importance of Rhodes in the naval history of the period was due no less to her commanding situation at this critical point than to the skill of her seamen. Both Demetrius and Ptolemy II probably really had 300 or more warships on their navy lists, a figure never reached by any other Power till the Roman Civil Wars, for Polybius' figures for the first Punic War are certainly too high[1]; and the fleet of Ptolemy II included so many great ships that it *may* have been of the average power of a quinquereme, an average never attained before or afterwards[2]. That in these circumstances Macedonia, with a much smaller fleet, defeated Egypt each time they met only illustrates once more that the man matters more than the ship.

[1] Tarn, *J.H.S.* xxvii, 1907, p. 48.
[2] Tarn, *Antigonos Gonatas*, App. x, p. 454.

But there were changes and developments in tactics. Given a fighting galley, there were two ways in which you could use it to attack the enemy; the weapon might be the ship itself, or the troops on board. The first method meant ramming, and then speed and skill in manœuvre were all-important, so as to take the enemy in flank; the second meant grappling and boarding, in which speed and skill mattered much less. Probably boarding was the oldest form of naval fighting, but after the advent of the trireme the two chief naval countries, Athens and Phoenicia, had come to believe in the ram; a trireme was so light that one blow might sink her, and her speed lent itself to manœuvre. With the invention of the quinquereme and her larger sisters the position began to alter again, for a quinquereme, besides being heavier, was normally slower than a trireme. These ships might survive several blows from a ram, even if they became waterlogged; also they could carry more troops. Phoenicia, Carthage, and to a certain extent Rhodes continued to trust to the ram, though it remained somewhat of a two-edged weapon, for it was easy enough to tear open your own bows; but boarding tactics gradually

gained ground. Even in the fifth century the
Dorian cities Corinth and Syracuse had believed in slower and heavier ships than the
Athenian, and were ready to ram prow to prow,
which Athenians avoided if they could; and
though much of the development is hidden from
us, we can see that by the middle of the third
century boarding tactics were in full swing; this
involved also ramming prow to prow, which
the heavier ships had no need to avoid. I do not
mean that the two tactics, the ram and boarding,
were mutually exclusive; everyone in the Hellenistic period had to use both; I mean that the
dominant tactics of a fleet had to be one or the
other. What settled the matter was the entry of
Rome and Macedonia into the naval arena; for
neither State had any tradition of naval skill,
while both possessed troops who, once they
could board, were tolerably certain of victory.
In the first Punic War the Roman sword beat
the Carthaginian ram. We cannot say for certain
that the contemporary struggle between Egypt
and Macedonia was a contest between ramming
and boarding; but we conjecture from Gonatas'
flagship *Isthmia* that Macedonia must have relied
on boarding, while the backbone of Egypt's

navy were the Phoenicians. Every cataphract had two decks, one beneath the rowers and one over their heads, on which stood the troops; but the *Isthmia* is called a three-decker. This can only mean that the troops also, like the rowers, were covered in, with a sort of deck over their heads, which shows their importance; Gonatas was imitating the way in which his father Demetrius had protected the crews of his siege machines. It seems obvious that a fleet led by such a vessel meant to board.

The best sailors of the time, the Rhodians, were ready to meet and employ every form of tactics, which is probably why they kept to quadriremes and quinqueremes. They used the ram if they could, and it is recorded that they continued to practise the Athenian *diecplus*, the deadly manœuvre in which the ships charged through the enemy line, disabling his oars, and then swung round and rammed him from the stern. But they did not shrink from a boarding fight, and were ready if necessary to ram prow to prow; an obscure statement in Polybius may perhaps imply that they had designed a form of prow and ram which forced the enemy's ram to strike them above and not below the waterline[1]; perhaps this was one of the secrets which they guarded so jealously. But they still cultivated speed—they could outrow anyone else[2]—and did not consider prow to prow ramming scientific; to prevent it they employed two poles projecting from the prow and carrying fire-baskets, which, if the enemy rammed prow to prow, fell on his deck and set him on fire; more than once we hear of the enemy ship flinching from the fire-baskets and thus exposing its side to the Rhodian ram. Others perhaps copied this, for a graffito of a ship with a fire-basket has been found in Egypt[3]. Philip V at Chios stopped the Rhodian *diecplus* by putting light Illyrian lembi between his cataphracts, and subsequently the use of a number of small vessels with a fleet became common; they correspond to the Liburnians of the Roman Imperial fleets,

[1] Polybius, XVI, 4, 12; the meaning is most obscure. I once thought it meant that they depressed their own bows; but apart from the difficulty of doing this in action (we do not know that a galley could take in water) it would not affect the enemy ram or make it give ἐξάλους πληγάς.

[2] *Ib.* XVI, 4, 4; Livy, XXXVII, 29, 9; 30, 2.

[3] *Bull. Soc. Arch. d'Alexandrie*, IV, 1902, facing p. 27; apparently late Ptolemaic. Botti, who published it, did not recognise what it was.

which were lembi under another name, but little is known of their functions in a fleet action; perhaps they attacked the oars of the bigger ships.

This question of attacking the oars is rather obscure. If you could, you rammed the enemy's oars and sawed your way through the bank; doubtless that is why Greeks invented their queer three-pronged ram. But unless you could save your own oars in some way, the enemy ship would also saw through *them* at the same time. I imagine they were drawn inboard sufficiently to clear the other ship's stem. Koester has a theory that they were thrown loose and left to swing back against the ship's side[1]; but with the huge many-handed oars the difficulty of mastering them again, with way on the ship, would I imagine be great, and also the oar-handle as it swung would brain the men next behind, unless all the rowers could be trained to fall flat at a signal, which I doubt. For one of the reasons for the adoption of the great oars was, that while a trireme could only do well if every man was skilled, in a quinquereme probably one skilled man to an oar would suffice, while the rest sup-

[1] *Seewesen,* p. 146.

plied weight and muscle—a parallel to what happened in the later phalanx. No State ever had all the skilled rowers it wanted.

Gonatas' device for protecting the troops on board was never followed up; perhaps it made the ship too heavy, or top-heavy. By the second century B.C. the troops were protected by light wooden turrets placed on the deck, and these remained in use throughout the period; if a beaten fleet was trying to escape, the turrets were thrown overboard. Besides the catapult, there was another machine which was *not* used on shipboard in battles—the boarding-bridge. Polybius' story that the Romans invented boarding-bridges in the first Punic War, used them at Mylae and Ecnomus with tremendous success, and then never used them again, is pure myth; what the ships did carry was some sort of grapnel. Boarding-bridges had in fact been invented by Diades 70 years before, and if a quinquereme had attempted to carry and use one in the way Polybius describes she would have turned turtle; a quinquereme could not even throw a grapnel without the rowers keeping their oars in the water to hold her steady— *stabiliendae causa* is Livy's phrase (XXXVI, 44, 8)

[149]

—and every rowing man will understand what sort of a ship that means.

Fleet tactics were influenced by land tactics; Salamis resembles Leuctra, Ecnomus is Cannae with the result reversed. Fleets sailed in line ahead and deployed into line abreast for battle; and as they hugged the coast whenever they could, a really decisive victory meant driving the enemy ashore, for effective pursuit at sea was impossible, rowers not being machines. The best victory recorded is that of Demetrius over Ptolemy I at Salamis in 306. Demetrius, whose right was inshore, was outnumbered, so he weakened his right and, like Epaminondas, greatly strengthened his left, the sea-wing; his left outflanked and crushed Ptolemy's right and he drove nearly his whole fleet ashore, capturing 120 ships out of 140. At Drepana, in the first Punic War, Adherbal with fewer ships drove most of the Roman fleet ashore, but the crews escaped. At Ecnomus the Carthaginians weakened their centre for the sake of making two powerful wings, as Hannibal did subsequently at Cannae, and attempted to close on both the Roman flanks; but the Roman centre broke through and together with the right wing drove the Cartha-

ginian left ashore, while the Roman left by grappling and boarding fought off the Carthaginian
right. Polybius' story that the Romans in this
battle advanced in the formation of a triangle is
quite impossible; no captains, let alone Roman
captains, could have kept station. What did
happen was that the Roman centre pressed forward, as at Cannae, but with better results. No
victories of the type of Salamis or Drepana are
recorded later, though Myonnesus in 190 B.C.,
in which Rome and Rhodes finally defeated
Antiochus III, was nearly one. The Syrian fleet
was so much the quicker in deploying from line
ahead into line abreast that the Romans were
already outflanked when the Rhodian admiral,
who had foolishly been placed in the rear and
was meant to come into line inshore, took the
matter into his own hands, came up at great
speed on the threatened flank, and saved the
situation.

The first battle represented as fought without
any tactics at all is that of Chios in 201, where
the Rhodians and Attalus of Pergamum defeated
Philip V; but I rather doubt Polybius' account
in this respect, and in particular it is difficult to
believe that Philip's great and disproportionate

SIEGE WARFARE & NAVAL WARFARE

loss in men was inflicted upon Macedonian troops in a mere *mêlée*. It was the Roman Civil Wars which brought the *mêlée* into prominence; the Roman idea now was to build heavier and stronger ships, cram them with legionaries, and have a land fight at sea. Two innovations are known; some ships now carried catapults, which the Hellenistic navies never did, and Octavian's admiral Agrippa used his catapults to fire grapnels[1]; and the larger ships of both Octavian and Antony had a sort of armour belt, formed of squared timbers bound together with iron[2], which made it difficult, or impossible, to ram them from the side. But, speaking generally, speed and skill both perished with the destruction of the Hellenistic states.

[1] Appian, *b.c.* v, 118.
[2] Plutarch, *Ant.* 66, σκάφεσι τετραγώνων ξύλων μεγάλων σιδήρῳ συνηρμοσμένων πρὸς ἄλληλα δεδεμένοις. Cf. Dio XLIX, 1, 2; L, 18, 5; 29, 1.

APPENDIX I

The Number of the Persian Cavalry

THE starting point for any guess at the total cavalry force of the Persian Empire under Darius III must be two figures derived from Hieronymus, which may be taken as accurate. In 323 Peithon obtained 8000 horse from the eastern satrapies (Diod. xviii, 7, 3) and after supplying these, the satraps of Persis and the east, in a contest which involved their own existence, could only raise another 4600 horse (Diod. xix, 14, 8); that makes 12,600 horse for everything east of the Tigris except Media and (perhaps) Susiana. The fact that, between the battles of Paraitakene and Gabiene, Eumenes, with Persis and the eastern satraps as his allies, was not able to increase his cavalry, though Antigonus, with Media to fall back upon, did increase his, shows that Persis and the east were pretty well drained dry. Arrian however (iii, 28, 8) gives Bessus 7000 horse for the defence of the satrapy of Bactria, the best cavalry district, though the course of the story shows that these did not necessarily all come from Bactria and Sogdiana. The figure is not necessarily as trustworthy as those of Hieronymus; but the 10,000 horse raised a century later by Euthydemus of

[153]

APPENDIX I

Bactria (Polyb. x, 49, 1), though off a larger territory, does support it, and I think Arrian must be taken to show that, in order to arrive at the *home defence* total under Darius III, we must raise Hieronymus' figure somewhat; there had of course been some loss in Alexander's battles, which may have fallen more heavily upon Persis than on other districts. Here we can only guess; but certainly a total of 20,000 horse for Persis and the eastern satrapies would seem to be an outside figure.

Hieronymus again gives a figure for Cappadocia, including Pontus and Paphlagonia: Eumenes in 321 raised 5000 horse (Diod. xviii, 30, 1 and 5; cf. Arr. τὰ μετὰ 'Αλέξανδρον, fr. 1, 27, Roos). The composition of the two cavalry wings at Gaugamela may show that Cappadocia, Armenia, and Syria (including Mesopotamia) were regarded as the equivalent of the far eastern satrapies, without Persis; certainly 15,000 for these countries would be generous. This makes a home defence total of 35,000, and there remain Media, Babylonia (of little account for cavalry), and western Asia Minor; I do not see therefore how the total can be over 45,000–50,000 horse. About three centuries later the tradition, for what it may be worth, gives the Parthian Empire 40,000 (Plut. *Ant.* 44) or 50,000 (Just. xli, 2, 6) horse off a much smaller territory, but with three centuries' increase of population and with practically no men subtracted for infantry.

I cannot see where a *higher* figure than 50,000 for

[154]

APPENDIX I

Darius III is to come from, and it may well be too high. Mr J. A. R. Munro has deduced from Herodotus that the paper total of the cavalry of Xerxes was 60,000 (*C.A.H.* IV, p. 272). Assuming this to be correct, we might, I suppose, imagine that the Indian provinces, lost before Darius III, figured on the list for at least 10,000 horse; looking at their dense population, this might be possible, but the Alexander story seems to show that the majority of the Indian peoples once in Persia's sphere fought on foot. It is perhaps more likely that the Xerxes figure was *only* a paper total, which could not have been realised in actual fact.

APPENDIX II

The Chinese evidence for the great war-horse

THE identification of the Nesaean horse with the great war-horse of Parthia (see p. 78, n. 1) can perhaps also be found from the Chinese side, in Ssu-ma Ch'ien's story, already mentioned, of how in 101 B.C. the Emperor Wu-ti got horses from Ferghana (Hirth, pp. 109 *sqq.*). There were two breeds in Ferghana, corresponding to the two types in Parthia; the horses which Wu-ti coveted, and which were "much stronger" than the Wusun horses, were the superior breed, and Hirth suggests (p. 141) that this must mean that the better breed had been imported from elsewhere; this can only mean Parthia. Now long ago T. de Lacouperie (*Western Origin of Chinese Civilisation*, pp. 220 *sq.*) transliterated the name of the capital city of Ferghana, which the Chinese attacked, as Nise, and suggested that the horses were Nisaean. This found little acceptance, and several other transliterations have been proposed (I noticed some, *J.H.S.* 1902, p. 281); but Hirth, who has always read the name Ir-shi, after a long discussion (pp. 141–2) now considers Nish a possible ancient equivalent of Ir-shi and inclines to agree with de Lacouperie in connecting Nish with the home of the Nisaean horses; he suggests that the word had come to be a technical term which was applied wherever good horses were bred. I would suggest myself, not "good horses," but one particular type of good horse, the great Nesaean-Parthian breed. (I apprehend that Nesaean, used by Strabo and Herodotus, is more correct than Nisaean; no connection is *known* between the horses and the old name Nisaea for part of Parthia-Hyrcania.)

I know of no representation as yet of the great war-horse in Parthian art; but it seems as if these horses can be traced in the art of China much earlier than in that of Iran (the Sassanian reliefs). It is obviously a matter on which I can only speak with every reserve, but certainly there are two distinct types of horse in the art of the Han dynasty, which may very well correspond to the two types in Ferghana and Parthia; and on the Shantung reliefs the great horse only appears in those of later date, which corresponds very well with Ssu-ma Ch'ien's story of the introduction of the great horse from Ferghana. The type of horse found in earlier Han art, though fairly strong and robust, is certainly not the great charger. It is seen in the horses figured in *Kin Shih So*, Vol. II, and on the bas-reliefs of Hiao T'ang-chan reproduced by E. Chavannes, *La sculpture sur pierre en Chine aux temps des deux dynasties Han*, 1893, Pls. XXXVI–XXXIX, and later in *Mission archéologique de la Chine septentrionale*, 1909, Pls. XXIV–XXIX; see also S. W. Bushell, *Chinese Art*, 2nd ed. 1910, Vol. I, Figs. 8–10, facing p. 27. (I owe these

APPENDIX II

references to the kindness of Mr R. L. Hobson of the British Museum.) These reliefs are of the first century B.C., that is, of a time when the great chargers introduced from Ferghana in 101 B.C. had not yet become common enough to influence art; and most of the horses are depicted in one conventional attitude. The sculptured horse of soon after 117 B.C. from the tomb of the general Houo K'in-ping, reproduced by Rostovtzeff, *Mon. Piot*, xxviii, 1925–6, pp. 161–3, seems, though rude, to belong to the same type; so, from their attitude, do the horses on a brick in the Sirén collection from a tomb of the Han period (*Ars Asiatica*, vii, 1925, *Documents d'art chinois dans la collection Osvald Sirén*, Pl. XXXIX, No. 570), though they are drawn as if somewhat lighter than the Shantung horses.

But on the later series of Shantung reliefs, from the tomb of the Wu family, second century A.D., we find quite a different type of horse, with enormous chests, barrels and hind quarters, very thick necks, and legs of an exaggerated fineness; except for the more slender legs, we have here the type of the Sassanian reliefs. There are a great number of figures of such horses (see especially Chavannes, *op. cit.* 1893, Pls. 10, 11, 14 *b*, 16, 17, 20, 20 *a*, 30 = *Mission archéologique*, Pls. L–LIII, LV *sqq.*); the old conventional attitude has been abandoned, and many forms of movement are depicted, some with much spirit. The best of such horses are perhaps those shown on Pl. XCVIII, No. 186, of *Mission archéo-*

APPENDIX II

logique; Han period, provenance unknown. The neck and chest of a little bronze horse of Han date in the Sirén collection (*op. cit.* Pl. X, No. 219) may suggest that, though a fantastic figure, it is derived from the great war-horse.

The great war-horse, of course far better portrayed, can easily be found among the clay horses of later date than the Han. There is a fine representation of such a horse, period of the Northern Wei (A.D. 386–535), in R. L. Hobson's *Catalogue of the Eumorfopoulos Collection*, Vol. I, Pl. XXI, No. 121, and a magnificent figure of one, T'ang period, in the Fitzwilliam Museum at Cambridge. The horses on the stele erected at Tchao Ling by T'ai Tsung, founder of the T'ang dynasty (*Mission archéologique*, Pls. CCLXXXVIII–CCXC, see Bushell, *op. cit.* Fig. 18), to commemorate six chargers he had ridden in battle, A.D. 618–626, are obviously of the same type; three are depicted galloping *ventre à terre* in the exact attitude of the galloping chargers on a third century Sassanian gem (Sarre, *Die Kunst des alten Persien*, Pl. CXLV). Figures in the Eumorfopoulos collection which may represent the same breed, perhaps slightly modified, in the T'ang period are Vol. I, Pl. XXIX, Nos. 288, 290; Pl. XXXIII, Nos. 239, 302.

APPENDIX III

Surenas' Camels

IT is of some importance for our knowledge of Surenas' organisation to know what his camels were, and the works I have met are either silent about camels in Iran or suggest that they were Bactrians. It seems certain that the camels known to Strabo (xv, 727) as domiciled about the Persian desert in the first century B.C., which had in fact been domiciled there for centuries (Herod. IX, 83; Xen. *Cyrop*, VI, 2, 8, VII, 1, 49; cf. *Hell.* III, 4, 24), were Arabian; this is shown by Alexander finding some there which had been bred for speed (Diod. XVII, 80, 3), an art which Arabs had long practised, as they still do (Herod. VIII, 86, as fast as horses; Aristot. *Hist. An.* IX, 48, 9, much faster than Nesaean horses). What clinches the matter, however, is that the *Ch'ien-han-shu* (*Annals of the Former Han*) relates that even in Bactria in the first century B.C. the Yueh-chi were using not the Bactrian camel but the one-humped, *i.e.* Arabian camel (A. Wylie, *Journ. Anthropol. Inst.* X, 1881, p. 40), which they can only have got from the Parthians. The camel of Iran was therefore the Arabian.

The slow-moving Bactrian camel had long been *domesticated*, as is shown by the bell round the neck of the one which has been brought as tribute on the frieze of Xerxes' palace at Persepolis (Perrot and

Chipiez, Vol. v, p. 805; Sarre, *op. cit.* Pl. XXVI); but the Persian artist has drawn it rather like an Arabian camel with two humps, which suggests that the Bactrian was to him a strange creature, while the Arabian was well known. Lucian's story (Προμ. εἰ ἐν λόγοις, 4) of Ptolemy I exhibiting a Bactrian camel *may* also show that it was a strange animal; but the story looks like an invention to explain the saying κάμηλος ἐν Αἰγυπτίοις. Where we do meet the Bactrian camel in Hellenistic times it is connected with India or China. The badly drawn Bactrian camel with an Oriental rider on a Greek vase figured by E. Saglio (Dar. Sagl. *s.v. camelus*) is said by him (from its context) to refer to Bacchus' Indian expedition; there is one on a coin of Menander in India (P. Gardner, *B.M. Coins, Greek and Scythic kings of Bactria and India,* Pl. XXXI, No. 10); and one with two riders on one of the before-mentioned Shantung bas-reliefs in China of the first century B.C. (Chavannes, *op. cit.* 1893, Pl. XXXIX = *Mission archéologique,* Pl. XXVII). I have not met with any representation of one in Iran except the one at Persepolis.

These facts seem to leave little doubt that Surenas' camels were Arabian, *i.e.* camels fast enough to accompany cavalry, whether he got them from Iran or from some Arab people. The Seleucids had employed an Arab camel-corps with swift camels (Livy, XXXVII, 40, 12); Surenas may have taken a hint from them, as the Palmyrenes did later, but he put the camels to another use.

APPENDIX IV

Δίκροτος *in a recent papyrus*

WHEN many years ago I wrote on the "Greek Warship" (*J.H.S.* 1905, pp. 137, 204), it appeared to me that the key to the understanding of what a trireme was could be found in the word δίκροτος. Given that δίκροτος was a triakontor, there was little difficulty in showing that it meant, not "double-beating," as had always been assumed, but "double-beaten," "double-welded" and referred to two horizontal squads of rowers, and consequently that a trireme had three horizontal squads, thranites astern, zugites amidships, thalamites in the bows; for details I must refer back to my paper. The proof however ultimately depended on the equation δίκροτος = triakontor, and that equation was a *deduction* from some passages in Arrian. It seemed to me, however, an inevitable deduction, and so I think it has turned out; for to-day the equation δίκροτος = triakontor can be based on a simpler foundation.

The papyrus in question is a Ptolemaic papyrus of the first century B.C. from Heracleopolis, and is Nos. 4 and 5 (two parts of one document) of the Heracleopolis papyri, all of the same time, published by W. Kunkel, *Archiv für Papyrusforschung*, VIII, 1927,

APPENDIX IV

pp. 169, 190. It deals with the despatch of rations of wheat for a number of ships, which are not at sea, but whose crews are doing liturgies for the *dioecetes* Athenaeus, and contains a list of ships and their trierarchs; the ration, reckoned in artabae, is for a period of eleven months. The papyrus is much broken, but the statement important for my purpose happens to be intact (first three lines of No. 5, transferred by Kunkel to make lines 20–22 of No. 4) and is a statement that from the total of artabae is to be deducted the ration already sent to the crew of one ship—ἀφ' ὧν τῶν ἐπεσταλμένων [read τὰ ἐπεσταλμένα, Kunkel] τῆι ϛ τοῦ 'Επεὶφ τοῖς ἐκ τοῦ Κλεονίκου τοῦ Ζεμίωνος δικρότου (πυροῦ) ψϛ. ψϛ must be a misprint for ψϛ; Kunkel in his commentary, p. 196, gives it as 706; also ψϛ is a *vox nihili*, for if it meant anything it would mean 900, and the papyri use the ordinary Greek sign for 900 (U. Wilcken, *Grundzüge*, p. xlv). Eleven months' ration for the crew of this δίκροτος was then 706 artabae. The artaba varied greatly in different parts of Egypt (Wilcken, *ib.* p. lxviii); but fortunately in this case another papyrus of the series, No. 8, l. 8, shows that at Heracleopolis at this time 2 artabae was a month's ration for one man; 706 is therefore eleven months' ration for 32 men. If Kunkel be right in his suggestion (he gives no reason) that 2 artabae a month is somewhat low, the number of men might be fewer; it cannot well be more.

Taking it at 32, we should suppose that this

APPENDIX IV

δίκροτος had 30 rowers and 2 officers, a κυβερνήτης and a πρῳρεύς; that is to say, it was a triakontor or something of about that size. Naturally an Athenian trireme, with its large crew, had a more elaborate list of officers; but that has no bearing on a little ship, while there is a curious passage in Diodorus which *does* bear on the matter—xIV, 43, 4, half of Dionysius' warships had πολιτικοὺς κυβερνήτας καὶ πρῳρεῖς ἔτι δὲ τοὺς ταῖς κώπαις χρησομένους, and the other half ξένους. Dionysius' ships were largely triremes, some perhaps even larger; this passage shows therefore that in Diodorus' own time (Augustus' reign) some sort of small ship with only rowers and these two officers was common, so common that Diodorus has transferred a customary parlance of his own time to the ships of an older day. There can be no doubt what this common species of small warship must have been; Diodorus had in mind the equipment of a Liburnian, and in fact Pseudo-Lucian (*Amores*, 6) equates δίκροτος with Liburnian (τῶν δικρότων οἷς μάλιστα χαίρειν Λιβυρνοὶ δοκοῦσιν), just as Hesychius (*s.v.* ἡμιολία) equates it with ἡμιολία. We see in fact that δίκροτος was a term which was applied to several kinds of small ships—triakontor, Liburnian, ἡμιολία; it was not a *ship*, but a method of arrangement. The δίκροτος of our papyrus had 15 rowers on each side, possibly less; this of course implies one-man oars. Now the *Etymologicum Magnum* (277, 1) says: δίκροτος ναῦς, ἡ δύο τοίχους ἐρετῶν ἔχουσα ὥσπερ τριήρης ἡ τρεῖς. The word τοίχους is of course corrupt; τοῖχος is a ship's side, and a trireme had not three sides. I shall not seek to emend the word, and it is not material; call it *x*. The passage then reads: "a δίκροτος has 2*x* of rowers just as a trireme has 3*x* of rowers," *x* having an identical value in each clause. How can one divide the rowers in a triakontor? Starboard and port oars are barred, a trireme not having three sides; the only possible division therefore is into fore and aft squads, horizontal squads. This is the natural thing in a small vessel; note how even a racing eight divides itself informally into stern four and bow four; and the two officers I have mentioned would (among other things) each have charge of one squad. *x* therefore is a horizontal squad, and the meaning of thranite, zugite and thalamite is as I have stated it. That ought to be the end of that impossible theory of superposed banks; but I have little hope that it will be.

I must notice Kunkel's commentary. Naturally he is somewhat at sea over δίκροτος, for, as he rightly says (p. 192), after referring to Torr and Koester, "die Literatur ist dürftig." And I have no idea whence he derived the extraordinary statement on p. 193, "Ein Fahrzeug mit dreissig Rudern muss doch wohl mindestens eine Bemannung von 40–100 Mann gehabt haben." The important point however is that he makes the ships of IV, ll. 13–16, δίκροτοι, and deduces from the artabae figures that a δίκροτος carried a crew of 65 to 80 men. There seems no reason for calling these ships δίκροτοι; the papyrus does not say *what* they were, and only one of the trierarch's names corresponds with a name in the list of δίκροτοι, v, ll. 18 *sqq.* (where the artabae figures are lost), the name Aphrodisios, which is extremely common (Preisigke, *Namenbuch*); this is not enough to go upon. It would however make no difference were he right; for δίκροτος is a term of *arrangement*, a twofold as opposed to a threefold division of rowers, and δίκροτοι were not necessarily all of one size; as regards Liburnians this is known. Meanwhile the passage I have commented on seems perfectly clear by itself, and I am grateful to Kunkel for publishing this papyrus.

INDEX

Abydos, siege of, 109, 119
Achaea, 10, 29, 30, 119
Achaemenids, 87–8
Achilles, 56–7
Actium, battle of, 31, 138
Adherbal, 150
Aeacides, 46
Aegospotami, battle of, 45
Aeneas Tacticus, 92, 102, 105
Aetolia, Aetolians, 2, 5, 10, 26, 46, 55–6
African elephant, 80, 94, 98–9
Agesilaus, 54
Agrianians, 21–2
Agrippa, 152
Alexander (the Great), 11–23, 27, 31, 37, 39–43, 55, 58–62, 64–6, 69–72, 85–6, 93, 97, 106, 109–12, 119–21, 130
Alexander of Pherae, 33, 56
Amorgos, battle of, 122
Anchimolius, 56
Antigonids, 27, 38, 133
Antigonus I, 18, 34–5, 38–40, 42, 45, 61–3, 97, 153
Antigonus II Gonatas, 44, 133, 135, 137–9, 145–6, 149
Antigonus III Doson, 36, 38, 48
Antiochus I, 96
Antiochus III, 27, 29, 41, 61, 66, 68, 76, 98, 143, 151
Antipater, 39
Antony, 39, 91, 120, 122, 136, 152
Aornos, 22, 119–20
Arabian camel, 90, 160–1
Arabs, 160–1
Arcadia, 9, 10

Archelaus, 36
Archimedes, 112, 116
Argos, 55
Argyraspids, 17
Armenians, 76, 86
Asclepiodotus, 13, 57
Asia Minor, 23, 143
Assyrians, 102–3, 105
Athens, Athenians, 4–6, 20, 40, 47, 56, 85, 105, 122, 131–2, 140, 143–5, 147, 164
Attalus I, 151

Babylonia, 38, 40, 48, 154
Bactria, Bactrians, 48, 153, 160
Bactrian camel, 160–1
Balearic islands, 20
Balkan pass, battle of the, 22
Bessus, 32–3, 64, 153
Bithynians, 54
Brasidas, 4
Byzantium, 45, 105

Cannae, battle of, 66–8, 150–1
Cappadocians, 71, 154
Cardaces, 65
Carrhae, battle of, 33, 86, 91–2
Carthage, Carthaginians, 26, 66, 94–6, 98–9, 102, 106, 115, 118, 144–5, 150–1
Cassander, 46
Celts, 12
Chabrias, 10
Chaeronea, battles of, 13, 33; 36
China, Chinese, 75, 77, 80–2, 156–9, 161
Chios, battle of, 123, 138, 147, 151

[167]

INDEX

[168]

INDEX

Labienus, 35
Lamian war, 47, 57, 131
Leosthenes, 47
Leuctra, battle of, 7, 150
Liburnians, 147, 164, 166
Libyan horses, 78, 81, 83
Livy, 127, 130, 149
Lucretius, 92
Lucullus, 76, 86
Lysander, 45
Lysimachus, 38, 41, 133–8, 141

Macedonia,Macedonians,11–18,
  23, 25, 27–30, 43–50, 57–9,
  61, 63, 95–6, 98, 101, 123,
  133, 143, 145
Machanidas, 120
Magnesia, battle of, 20, 29,
  61–2, 66, 68, 76, 100
Malta, 125, 127
Mantinea, battle of, 33, 36, 119
Maracanda, 19, 40
Marathon, battle of, 40, 52
Marcellus, 112, 121
Mardonius, 53
Massaga, 13, 18, 111
Massagetae, 74, 86
Mazaeus, 84
Media, 153–4
Megalopolis, siege of, 85, 95,
  106, 109
Melitaea, 108
Memnon, 134, 141
Mithridates I of Parthia, 48
Mithridates Eupator of Pontus,
  30
Motye, siege of, 102
Munda, battle of, 35
Myonnesus, battle of, 151

Nabis, 47
Nesaean horses, 78–81, 156–7,
  160

Numidians, 67

Olympias, 46
Olynthus, siege of, 21

Paeonians, 58
Palazzo Spada ship, 136
Panormus, 96
Paraitakene, battle of, 18, 34–6,
  62–3, 67, 97, 153
Parmenion, 64, 67
Parthia, Parthians, 33, 48, 72,
  74–9, 83–91, 100, 154, 156–7,
  160
Pegasus, 78, 82–3
Peithon, 71, 153
Pelopidas, 33, 56
Perdiccas, 39, 71, 95
Pericles, 101
Perinthus, siege of, 103
Perseus, 17, 29, 134
Persia, Persians, 10, 32, 51–5,
  63–5, 70, 73, 85, 87, 153–5
Persian Guard, 61, 64–5
Persis, 42, 153–4
Pharnabazus, 54
Philip II, 7, 11, 13, 20, 33, 40,
  102–3, 105–6
Philip V, 25, 27, 29, 38, 40, 44,
  107, 109, 133, 147, 151
Philopoemen, 33, 36
Philostratus, 56, 79
Phoenicia, Phoenicians, 102–3,
  106, 130, 132, 144, 146
Phthiotic Thebes, 107
Pissuthnes, 9
Plataea, battle of, 52–3, 87
Pliny, 79, 106, 132
Polybius, 44, 68, 99, 111, 127,
  140, 143, 146, 149, 151
Polyperchon, 45–6, 57, 95, 106,
  109
Porus, 18, 22, 70, 93, 97

[169]

INDEX

CAMBRIDGE: PRINTED BY
W. LEWIS, M.A.
AT THE UNIVERSITY PRESS

For EU product safety concerns, contact us at Calle de José Abascal, 56–1°, 28003 Madrid, Spain or eugpsr@cambridge.org.

 www.ingramcontent.com/pod-product-compliance
Ingram Content Group UK Ltd.
Pitfield, Milton Keynes, MK11 3LW, UK
UKHW012343130625
459647UK00009B/486